YOUR COMPLETE STRESS-PRO

A practical guide to overcoming s
through relaxation therapies, includi
breathing and healing techniques.

By the same author
ABOUT LAETRILE
ACUPUNCTURE TREATMENT OF PAIN
AMINO ACIDS FOR THERAPY
AN END TO CANCER?
CANDIDA ALBICANS: Could Yeast Be Your Problem?
INSTANT PAIN CONTROL
NEURO-MUSCULAR TECHNIQUE
OSTEOPATHY
SELF HELP FOR HIGH BLOOD-PRESSURE
YOUR COMPLETE STRESS-PROOFING PROGRAMME
YOUR OWN SLIMMING AND HEALTH PROGRAMME

YOUR COMPLETE

Stress-Proofing Programme

How to Protect Yourself Against the Ill-Effects of Stress

Including Relaxation and Meditation Techniques

by

LEON CHAITOW
N.D., D.O., M.B.N.O.A.

Illustrated by Bevil Roberts

THORSONS PUBLISHERS LIMITED
Wellingborough · New York

Published in the U.K. by Thorsons Publishers Ltd., Denington Estate,
Wellingborough, Northants NN8 2RQ and in the USA by
Thorsons Publishers Inc., 377 Park Avenue South, New York 10016.
Thorsons Publishers Inc. are distributed to the trade by
Inner Traditions International Limited, New York.

First published 1983
This edition first published 1984
Second Impression 1985
Third Impression 1986

British Library Cataloguing in Publication Data

Chaitow, Leon
    (Relaxation and meditation techniques).
    Your complete stress-proofing programme.
    1. Stress (Psychology)   2. Stress (Physiology)
    3. Self-care, Health
    I. Title   II. Your complete stress-proofing programme
    616.8   BF 575.S75

ISBN 0-7225-0983-9

Printed in Great Britain by
Richard Clay (The Chaucer Press) Ltd,
Bungay, Suffolk

Contents

To my darling wife, Alkmini, whose help and support made the writing of this book possible.

Acknowledgements

In the text, reference is made to numerous researchers and writers whose work I have distilled into the sections on the treatment of stress. I wish to express my gratitude to all of these people. In particular, I would like to record my gratitude to the late Bagnell Goodwin, who first kindled my interest in the importance of 'stress-proofing' when I was a student at the British College of Naturopathy and Osteopathy between 1956 and 1960.

Introduction

The aim of this book is to present a choice of methods, the application of which will better enable you to cope with stress. Stress itself therefore needs to be looked at, for it comes in a variety of shades and shapes. Once we understand the diverse nature of stress, and also its possible ramifications in terms of ill health and disturbed function, the importance of these methods will become apparent.

Watches used to be described as 'waterproof'. This has now been altered to 'water-resistant' where applicable. In stating the degree of resistance, the manufacturers have, of course, to pay due attention to both the nature of the hazard and the properties and qualities of the instrument. Such aspects would include consideration of the variations in water (salt, fresh, acid, alkaline, etc.) and also the materials and design of the watch. Finally, the watch is guaranteed resistant to water up to a certain depth (30 metres, 50 metres etc.). There are other hazards facing wrist watches, such as shock, intense heat, cold, magnetism etc. In the same way, the human condition faces a range of stress factors and it is not possible to 'stress-proof' anyone, absolutely. However, stress-resistance can be increased and, as in the case of the watch, attention needs to be paid to both the stress factors and all their variables as well as the instrument at risk, the human machine. The aim is therefore not to eliminate stress, but to modify it where possible and to encourage appropriate responses to it.

Health and ill health are the result of the complex inter-relationship between the unique individual and the challenges and stresses of his particular internal and external environment. Stress can be a self-produced phenomenon (e.g. anger, fear) or it can be externally generated (e.g. job insecurity, an unstable marriage etc.). More usually, the stress-picture is an amalgam of internally and externally originating factors. Attitudes, beliefs, behaviour patterns, personality traits and deeply entrenched habits of thought may all be partly responsible, and several ways of examining and modifying such factors will be discussed. The importance of correct nutrition, sufficient exercise and rest, as well as such factors as adequate access to full spectrum light (daylight) will be touched on in as much as they relate to stress reduction and to our aim of stress-proofing the body. These areas are important, but the main point of this book is to show that there are defences which can be erected against stress whatever form it takes and that, by the regular application of these methods, great benefit can be derived in terms of health and well-being. We must certainly aim at reducing stress, but must also increase our resistance to it and learn to counteract its effects.

In brief, therefore, we shall examine some of the major causes of stress. This will be followed by a look at the physiological and pathological effects which prolonged stress can produce. Reference will be made to the relationship that exists between all changes in lifestyle (marriage, divorce, job changes etc.) and subsequent ill health. Knowing what constitutes stress can certainly alert us as to desirable evasive action and some consideration will be given to the roles in stress reduction of diet, exercise, rest, light etc., as well as positive suggestions relating to the changing of attitudes and coming to an understanding of those aspects of stress which are within our conscious control.

Finally, a number of different relaxation methods, as well as a selection of meditation techniques will be presented, together with a résumé of current thinking on the use of mind/body therapies, such as visualization, which stress the power of the mind in promoting good health. The power of the mind to create a disturbed physiology and actual disease, is matched by its equal ability to create health and harmony. A variety of techniques exist in this field, some more suited to a particular person than others. The main aim of this book is to enable the reader to find those methods that best suit him or her and to explain how important their regular use is in regaining and maintaining health. Whether active or passive relaxation methods are employed, or whether meditation alone is found to produce the desired results, is immaterial. What matters is that we learn to harness the mind's latent force towards positive rather than negative goals, and that the mind/body complex is insulated, as far as possible, from those internally and externally generated stresses which, left unchecked, will first weaken, then cripple and finally destroy the body.

Health and disease and all the grey area between, are states which reflect the ability, or otherwise, of the body to maintain equilibrium (known as homeostasis) in the face of a host of environmental threats and hazards. At any given time, the individual represents a culmination of all that has been inherited, and all that has been acquired and developed up to that moment. The degrees of susceptibility and of resistance that the body can demonstrate, will be absolutely unique to him. With so many variables, it should be obvious that no one method, system or prescription can apply to everyone, even if similar outward manifestations of ill health are evident. For this reason, less emphasis should be placed on signs, symptoms and outward manifestations of ill health; whilst these are important, especially to the individual, they do not indicate more than the particular manner in which his organism has responded to those factors which have threatened him. The same symptoms (e.g. headache) can result from a variety of causes. The same apparent cause (e.g. anxiety regarding work) can produce quite different symptoms, say insomnia in one person, palpitations in another and headaches in a third.

Treatment of the symptoms can never bring more than short-term benefit. To remove the symptom and ignore the cause is patently wrong, for that or another symptom will surely manifest itself sooner or later. Only by improving the general level of function of the total organism and by removing, where possible, the causes of the condition, can a successful outcome be anticipated. Since causes of anxiety are often outside the control of the individual ('Will there be a third World War?'; 'Will the factory close down?'; 'How will I pay my bills?', etc.), it is necessary to provide ways of altering the ways in which such problems are viewed. In addition, techniques are necessary whereby, even if such stress remains to some extent constant, the individual can nullify and counteract its ill effects by positive action. This is where relaxation, meditation and other exercises of the mind come in.

The individuality of each person must be recognized; this leads to a realization that the particular factors which enable successful adaptation to the environment will vary. Stress-proofing involves gaining understanding and insight into the nature of the problems of stress, as well as a determination to make changes, alterations, modifications and efforts in accordance with this knowledge. Through this apparent maze, I would urge the reader to hold fast to one concrete thought: given the chance, the body is a self-healing, self-repairing and self-regenerating organism. The aim is to give it that chance, and at the same time to erect barriers which will provide protection against future hazards.

1.
The Causes and Nature of Stress

Stress-induced illnesses have now replaced infectious diseases as the most prevalent health afflictions affecting the industrialized nations. Many of these illnesses, including arthritis, cardiovascular disease, respiratory disease, cancer, depression etc., seem to be associated both with stress (and other factors), and particular types of personality. Aspects of the equation require attention of course, and stress reduction and stress-proofing, as well as personality or behavioural modification, all present ways in which the individual can evade the consequences of stress.

Stress can be seen to be most harmful when there is an inappropriate response to it. When, for example, a man strolling in a field is confronted by a charging bull, his sprint to the nearest gate can be seen to be entirely appropriate as a response to the stress factor. He judged and matched the required response and no ill effects would result from the incident. On the other hand, the individual's judgement of what is an appropriate response may be faulty, for example when anger is generated and maintained in response to a minor incident. Attitudes, beliefs and habitual patterns of behaviour can be seen to be the arbiters of whether the individual responds appropriately to a particular stress factor and, therefore, of whether there is consequent harm in terms of physiological stress.

There are a number of defensive tricks which the mind can play in response to any challenge or stress. These include repression of thoughts and memories which might prove stressful, as well as 'rationalization', in which the individual makes up an account of his behaviour in response to stress, the true explanation of which would produce anxiety. Such common defences, if producing anxiety states or personality changes, require professional psychotherapy to provide insights into and a resolution of the problem.

It is self-evident then, that what is to one individual, a major stress factor, may to another be only a minor irritant. The difference lies in the individual's attitude towards the stress factor. For one person, for example, the meeting of a deadline, the need to be at a particular place at a fixed time, is of vital importance, and the prospect of being late, of failing to meet the deadline, generates a great deal of tension and anxiety (i.e. stress). To another person, such deadlines are mere guidelines, and no particular worry is felt at their being missed.

Attitudes depend upon the individual's concept of reality. The world as he sees it is his own reality, and when this comes into conflict with the external environment, stress results. To some extent, all change represents stress. Anything that calls upon the mind-body totality (the individual) to adjust or change from that which is normal, represents stress. The individual's concept of what is normal, what is right, how things ought to be, is therefore the sounding board on which the external environmental factors operate. Beliefs and attitudes often determine the degree of stress, anxiety etc. experienced. For example, the death of someone close is undoubtedly a major stress factor, and yet to someone whose beliefs include a certainty of an after-life or of reincarnation, the death will be seen as part of a continuous process, not an end, and therefore the amount of stress will be minimized.

It has been possible to grade the potential of events or changes in an individual's life. In the following chart, scores have been allotted to each event so that the degree of susceptibility to the effects of stress can be estimated. This can be valuable in alerting individuals to pay extra attention to dealing with those elements of health maintenance which are within their control. Some such methods will be dealt with in Chapter 5.

Stress and Changes in Lifestyle
This scale is based on the work of T. H. Holmes and R. H. Rahe (*Journal of Psychosomatic Research*, 1967, No. 11) and is meant as a guide to the assessment of measurable stress factors, resulting

from having to adjust to change. There are many other sources of stress, but it is true to say that a high score on this chart (300 or more) over a short time-span (six months or so), is a strong indicator (affecting 80 per cent of people) of the likelihood of major illness becoming apparent. If the score is relatively high, anything from 150 to 299 points, about 50 per cent of people become ill soon afterwards, and if under 150 points are scored, fewer than 30 per cent become ill. The higher the score, the greater the need for stress-proofing.

Changes in Lifestyle	Scale
Death of husband or wife	100
Divorce	73
Marital separation	65
Jail sentence or being institutionalized	63
Death of close member of family	63
Illness or injury	53
Marriage	50
Loss of job	47
Reconciliation with marriage partner	45
Retirement	45
Health problem of close member of family	44
Pregnancy	40
Sex problems	39
Addition to family	39
Major change at work	39
Change of financial status	39
Death of friend	37
Change in line of work	36
Change in number of marital arguments	35
Large mortgage taken out	31
Mortgage or loan foreclosed	30
Responsibility change	29
Child leaves home	29
In-law problems	29
Personal achievement realized	28
Wife starts or stops work	26
Starting at new school	26
Leaving school	26

Change in living conditions	25
Change in personal habits	24
Trouble with employer	23
Change in working hours	20
Change in residence	20
Change in recreation	19
Change in church activities	19
Change in social activities	18
Small mortgage taken out	17
Change in sleeping habits	16
Change in number of family get-togethers	15
Major change in eating pattern	15
Holiday	13
Christmas	12
Minor violation of law	11

It is known that these scores and the position on the scale of some of the incidents, vary in different cultures. Different belief systems place the stress of marriage higher in Europe, for example, than in Japan. It is also clear from the list that stress factors are not necessarily unpleasant episodes. A holiday for example is seen as a cause of stress. Change itself, pleasant or unpleasant, is therefore one potential for stress. But it can be argued that since even in high-scoring individuals, 20 per cent do not become ill soon afterwards, it is the response of the individual, his attitudes, beliefs and underlying health status, that is the real determining factor in the effects of stress. This list can be used as a guide, but it should be coupled with thoughts as to what are the most appropriate, least stressful, responses; these responses should then be cultivated.

There is another element in life, which can often produce even more stress than events and changes which actually take place. This is the highly charged area of anticipated problems or events. Whilst losing a job is indeed a high-scoring stress factor, the anticipation of such a loss presents potentially greater stresses by virtue of the time-scale involved. Once a job has been lost, the reality of the situation determines that the individual does something about the matter. Looking for a new job, making practical arrangements regarding finance etc. are all stressful but are, in fact, responses to the event. If, however, there are rumours of possible redundancy, and the anxiety and uncertainty continues for months or years, then the stress induced may be far greater. It is nevertheless worth remembering that, in such a case, there are practical steps which can be taken to minimize the effects of the stress once the individual realizes what is happening.

So, apart from actual changes in life being potentially stressful, it is also evident that anticipation of such changes (i.e. projecting from the present into possible future happenings) also creates stress. It is also, unfortunately, true that much stress relates to an inability to resolve events which are in the past. Guilt, self-pity, brooding over past events, real or imagined, therefore present another major area of stress production. Not only does such attention to the past produce stressful changes in the body, but it greatly diminishes the individual's ability to function well in the present.

Those factors which have a potential for allowing stress may be seen as real physical events, such as intense noise, extreme heat or cold, or as real, anticipated or remembered unpleasant events, such as divorce; in addition, any change from the status quo, such as a visit, a holiday or promotion at work are likely to involve some stress. Such factors can be termed 'stressors', and the potential for harm of all of these will be tempered by attitudes, emotions and personality factors. Conflicts, real or imagined, between the individual and other people or groups is a further major stress factor. The strain, conflict and pressure, resulting from any variety of stressors, may produce an anxiety state which may be short-lived or long-term, depending upon underlying personality traits, acquired attitudes, beliefs and so on. Since it is not possible, in the main, to protect oneself against the major changes in life, it should be thought of as desirable and necessary that attitudes should be cultivated which will minimize the effects of the inevitable vicissitudes of life.

External stress factors, whilst easy to identify, are less easy to measure and control. These might include excessive noise (engineering workers); exposure to excessive heat (bakers), or cold (workers in cold-storage areas); intensely boring or repetitive occupations (assembly line workers), and such factors as commuting on an unreliable transport system, or having to drive in heavy traffic for hours every day. Other, more extreme, examples of constant external stress factors are those endured by people working in areas of potential danger (police, soldiers, deep-sea divers), or of particularly unnatural working conditions (miners, oil-rig workers) etc. The body responds to all such stresses in accordance with a predictable pattern of internal changes. Stress is, however, cumulative, and a relatively minor event, when added to a large existing stress load, will often prove to be more than the body's adaptation processes can cope with. To a large extent, the breaking point can be avoided by taking care of that aspect of the stress jigsaw puzzle, most easily alterable, i.e. the personal habits, and life-style, of the individual. A change in attitude can dramatically alter the potential for damage, created by externally generated stress, but such a change is far more difficult to achieve than, for example, an improvement in rest, exercise, sleep and nutrition.

From childhood onwards, stress provides a spurt and incentive to development. The will to please others and to satisfy inner drives, are responses to needs, desires and targets or goals, set by authority, society, family, self, etc. This aspect of stress is vital to human survival and development. It is when there are inappropriate responses to such drives that stress becomes potentially harmful. Whether considering early childhood development, schooling, family life, courtship, marriage, higher education, work or retirement, life presents a kaleidoscope of stressful events, challenges, obstacles, pitfalls and sometimes tragedies. The ground on which these events fall is the personality and make-up of the individual, and since the avoidance of all stressful events and stages in life is not possible, it is this ground, the personality and belief system, that presents the main opportunity for modification, and consequent lessening of the impact of stressors

Cardiologists, Friedman and Rosenmann, have described the 'type A' personality who is predisposed to heart disease. The type A individual moves, walks, talks and eats quickly. He finds it difficult to relax, sets himself deadlines, often undertakes more than one task at a time; he fidgets, is ambitious, and so on. The 'type B', who is much less prone to heart disease, is a direct contrast; this type moves, talks and eats slowly, is able to relax; is unambitious, avoids pressure and deadlines etc. None of this is too surprising, but what is exciting is that, when motivated (often by an early coronary), the type A can turn into a type B, by altering his behaviour, to actually copy type B mannerisms until they become habitual. There is a consequent drop in the likelihood of coronary disease following such a modification. Type A will have then adopted more desirable and appropriate responses to the needs of life, and will have enhanced his chances of long-term survival.

It is now evident that living in the present lessens the tendency to dwell on past or future events, or on anticipated events. A further aspect of this is that the nearer the individual's concept of reality is to actual life, the less stress there will be created. Reality may not always be the same for all people, but in many daily situations, the stress felt by people is the direct result of their 'fantasy', of how things should be, being at odds with reality. My 'fantasy', for example is that when people make appointments they ought to keep them, and what is more, they ought to be on time. In reality, however, this is often not the case. The annoyance and stress which is generated every time an appointment is missed and someone is late, could be avoided if I could bring my fantasy closer to real life, i.e. anticipate that people will, by the nature of things, be late for or will actually forget to keep their appointments from time to time.

In terms of attitudes to life and events, such thoughts or phrases as 'if only . . . ' or 'it should have been like . . . ', or 'wouldn't it have been nice if . . . ' indicate a failure to accept reality or an unwillingness to accept what has actually happened. This type of 'fantasy' may appear harmless, but it is as potentially stressful as dwelling in the past or future. It is, in fact, another facet of that same tendency. 'Be there now' is the best piece of advice for such an individual to bear in mind. Life is in the 'here and now'. In the past, the future and the 'if only' lie shadows, demons and stress. Nowhere is this more evident than in personal relationships, whether this be at work or in the home environment. Much stress results from an inability to express feelings clearly, without becoming upset. If feelings are expressed inadequately, then hostility and anger will often develop. Once again, many such stresses relate to differences of opinion as to what is, and what is not reality. Interpersonal relationships require that individuals express their feelings clearly and in a non-hostile manner, and that they are then prepared to listen to a similar expression of the other individual's views, without feeling 'got at' or under attack. This is the ideal of course, and it may be difficult to achieve because of long-held attitudes and firmly-rooted personality traits, but it is, undoubtedly, the way to ensure non-stressful relationships. Seeing reality in the present, the ability to deliver unbiased, non-hostile expressions of opinion, and the ability to listen are, then, qualities to be cultivated.

In personal relationships, much tension is generated as a result of unfulfilled expectations. If one party anticipates a gesture or form of recognition (such as a birthday card or telephone call), which does not materialize, a tense and resentful attitude may ensue. Again, an ability to communicate can defuse such a situation. Errors or sins of omission are just as potentially stressful as sins of commission; i.e. non-events as opposed to actual events. If bottled up and nursed, such feelings can produce stress out of all proportions to the importance of the actual incident.

The range of possible stress factors is almost endless, and the possible permutations of reaction to them, equally so. It has been said that there are only two basic emotions, 'like' and 'dislike'. All other emotions stem from variations and degrees of these prime feelings. The amazing differences in individuals, tastes, likes, dislikes and so on, makes it obvious that there is seldom any intrinsic quality in an event, object or situation, which guarantees it being universally liked or disliked (one man's meat is patently another man's poison). It is also worth noting that at different stages in life and under different conditions, the same individual's 'likes' and 'dislikes' will vary. The conclusion may be drawn that the individual can possibly be taught, or can teach himself, to like what was previously disliked, and vice versa. Thus if, because of degrees of 'liking' or 'disliking', a person's behaviour gives rise to a more stressful existence and more problematic relationships than are desirable, reduction of stress is possible only through a basic change in attitudes. Just as type A must change from a fast-moving, fast-talking, fast-acting, fast-eating individual to one with more deliberate habits, so must the individual who says 'that's how I am, I can't change!' be made to understand that change is not only possible but desirable, and that self-interest dictates that it should be so. Changing habits and attitudes is merely a matter of understanding and recognizing them for what they are, followed by modifications in behaviour. This is easily said and, obviously, not as easily achieved. However, as will become clear, the alternatives to such behavioural modification may often be serious illness.

In considering behavioural modification – the changing of habitual attitudes and ways of responding, it is important to realize that whenever we behave in a particular manner, we reinforce the belief that lies behind that form of behaviour. If there is always an angry tantrum in response to real or imagined criticism, then the individual's belief that this is the appropriate response will be reinforced by each such outburst. To alter the underlying belief requires an altered response. By substituting a less stressful, less provocative reaction, the belief will develop, and be reinforced that the new reaction is correct and appropriate. Obviously, in interpersonal relation-ships, two such modified responses may be needed and this is not easy to arrange. Once the individual realizes the role that habit plays in reinforcing undesirable modes of behaviour, it is possible to begin to change. By acting in a manner in which the other person is dealt with as you would wish to be dealt with yourself, and by expressing whatever needs to be said honestly and calmly, the opportunity will grow for a less stressful relationship. Such behaviour changes often spark changes for the better in the other half of the relationship.

It is worth noting that no-one and nothing makes you angry. You do it all on your own. Such feelings are always self-generated, and this is true of most emotions. We choose to be angry, jealous, guilty, bitter, etc. and, equally, we choose to be happy, giving, loving, etc. Our attitudes and behaviour can be self-modified, and most experiences present a choice of response – one negative and stressful and the other positive and, potentially, offering the opportunity for growth and self-knowledge – the choice remains with the individual. Attention to the stress-reducing measures presented in later chapters, becomes a clear matter of whether the individual is prepared to accept responsibility for his life and action, or not.

Stress is cumulative. Whilst, in early life, most people can cope with a great deal of emotional and physical trauma, this facility diminishes as life progresses. There are, of course, inherited characteristics which will influence every individual's particular capacity for coping. There are other factors which will also, to varying degrees, determine to what extent stress can influence the individual's physical and mental health. Among these are nutritional considerations, structural factors, exercise patterns, general fatigue, and the sum total – long-term and in the recent past – of stress. These influences will become clearer in later chapters. At this stage, it is worth noting that stress is the spur that moves man to action, and that, if responses are not appropriate, it can also become the boulder that crushes him.

There is indeed a point at which the body's capacity for adjusting to and adapting in the face of stress becomes inadequate. When this occurs, health begins to break down in obvious ways. This will be dealt with in the next chapter, in greater detail, but it is important to note that this very noticeable deterioration in health is itself a potent stressor. Anxiety in the face of changes in function, the onset of pain etc., quickens the downward spiral. If the individual waits for this stage before undertaking reforms, he may have waited too long. It is still often possible to regain health at this stage, but only with great effort.

There are extrinsic factors which are outside the individual's control, but there are also many aspects of the picture which are controllable. There are, of course, states of mind which generate stress, which are outside the conscious control of the individual. There are many deep-seated anxiety states and depressions, in which only skilled psychotherapy and counselling will enable the individual to achieve insights and understanding and ultimately, a resolution of his problem. Such forms of treatment lie outside the scope of this book, but it is suggested that the general principles outlined here and the techniques described can only be of help, even in such cases. However, no-one who is receiving psychotherapy should attempt self-treatment without first consulting his practitioner.

2.
The Physical Effects of Stress

Stress is an essential and constant part of life. It is the spur that drives man to all achievement. When excessive, it can also destroy him. All the ages and stages of life are transitional; from baby to toddler, from schoolchild to young adult, from active worker to retired pensioner and so on. Likewise, all change has potential stress implications which, overlayed upon the external and internal stresses of living, are constantly affecting the mind and body of the individual.

One definition of stress, given by the great researcher into this ubiquitous phenomenon, Dr Hans Selye, is simply 'the rate of wear and tear on the body'. All change requires adaptation on the part of the organism. If we go from a warm room into the freezing cold outdoors, adaptive mechanisms immediately become operative to help the body to maintain its equilibrium. Adaptive processes take place in response to all changes and stressors, whether these are physical, such as heat and cold, chemical, such as polluted water and air, drugs, or self-generated emotions such as anger, grief or joy. Anything that is perceived as threatening the mind or body, arouses a response of an adaptive or defensive nature instantly. This ability to attempt to maintain the safe equilibrium of the body is known as homeostasis. It is, for a variety of reasons, not always successful. The biochemistry of the body may be inadequate for the task, perhaps through faulty nutrition, and this and other possible factors, including structural integrity, will be considered later. If the response is inadequate, or if perception of threats is inaccurate, then unbalanced and faulty body adjustments may occur with harmful consequences.

The normal stress reaction is seldom the result of the outside agency, but rather it is the system's reaction to it.

Whether the stressor is physical, such as sudden exposure to cold, or psychological, such as a sudden crisis or a change of responsibility at work, unpleasant news, etc., the body begins to make biochemical changes in response to its perceived needs. Such changes take place almost constantly throughout life to a greater or lesser degree. If a stressor is prolonged, continuous or extreme in its nature, then the defensive mechanisms of the body become even more active. In response to intense heat, changes take place in the blood chemistry and circulatory system in order to cool the body by means, for example, of extra fluid loss and evaporation through the skin. Should this fail to achieve the desired effect, then an even greater defensive effort might involve fainting and temporary unconsciousness, in order to reduce all bodily functions to a minimum. Such homeostatic efforts, though, fall short of being actual stress reactions, unless prolonged.

In response to any stress or extreme, the body undergoes a series of changes which Selye has grouped under the heading of the 'fight or flight' reaction. Quite logically, the response to being confronted with real physical danger, such as the appearance of a man-eating animal, would be to attack it or to escape from it. Whichever was the choice, the body would require instantly available energy, strength, concentration, etc. There would be no time for slow deliberation or stages of progressive arousal, for by that time the adversary would be commencing its meal! If an appropriate response (fight or flight) to the stressor were forthcoming, then the biochemical and other changes triggered by the initial shock, would be utilized, and no ill effects would be felt.

Today, people are seldom faced, on a daily basis, with such life and death stress situations. However, the mind and body may be felt to be threatened in many other ways than by a man-eating tiger. Any perceived (accurately or not) threat or danger to the mind or body will produce a similar 'fight or flight' reaction, and there may be ways of producing an appropriate response to these. For instance, someone might say something which is perceived as being insulting, hurtful etc. The stress reaction, which includes a tensing of the muscles as well as biochemical (hormonal and other) changes, could simply be 'bottled up' and remain as an extra degree of muscular tension. If a suitable verbal and/or physical response were to be found, however, then again the preparation for action would have been expressed and used, and no ill effects would result. The degree of stress imposed on the body will vary with the individual's perception of what constitutes a threat – one man would laugh and shrug off an insult, another would reach for his gun! It will also vary with the individual's ability to respond appropriately. One man would calmly but firmly state his views and inform the villain of the piece of his feelings. Another would bluster and fluster and add fuel to the fire, and not obtain psychological release from the hurt and anger within. The stress factor, therefore, cannot be seen as the main determinant of the degree of 'fight or flight' reaction, but only as its potential trigger. The harm done to the body by prolonged, repeated arousal, is largely an outcome of the individual's beliefs, attitudes, personality and ability to see objectively what constitutes real, and what constitutes imagined danger, physically or mentally.

The actual processes that take place during arousal and 'fight or flight' reactions are quite amazing to contemplate. It is possible to extrapolate these immediate changes and to see their potential for major physical damage if they are repeated or prolonged. The following process occurs instantly within the body in response to stress: the muscles tense in preparation for activity; the hypothalamus (part of the brain) co-ordinates a number of hormonal changes; the pituitary gland is activated, and among other results of this is the production by the adrenal glands of the hormones, adrenaline and noradrenaline. As a result, a vast number of bodily changes occur; the pupils of the eye dilate – no doubt to see more clearly; the heart pumps more rapidly to service the extra requirements of the tense muscles and this increases the blood pressure; the extra blood for the muscles requires extra oxygen, and the respiratory rate therefore quickens to cope with this, as well as to help expel additional waste products resulting from increased activity. Blood being diverted to potential muscular activity requires the shut-down of some other functions, including reduction in blood through the kidneys, as well as the ceasing of digestive functions. To this end, saliva dries up and the intestines and stomach stop working. The body's need for additional energy is met by the liver releasing stored glucose into the blood stream, where the oxygen changes it into readily available energy. In anticipation of extra activity, the skin cools the body down by opening its pores to encourage perspiration. Since blood is being diverted to the muscles, there is a tendency for the skin to become paler. There may be involuntary urination or defecation, due to an over-reaction of that part of the nervous system responsible for restoring the status quo (the parasympathetic nervous system); normally, however, the sphincters controlling these functions close to prevent any further activity until the crisis is past. Other aspects of the body's defence capability, the immune system, becomes less active during such arousal. This makes infection more likely at such a time. Since the muscles are tense, they will be producing lactic acid break-down products, which have the effect of re-inforcing the anxiety and tension felt by the individual. This list of activities is by no means fully comprehensive, but it should give an idea of what a devastating effect prolonged stress has on the normal body functions.

In the initial stages of arousal, most systems adapt to and accommodate such changes. After arousal there is a return to the status quo, especially if the response is adequate. However, if arousal is repeated over and over again, then some of the changes mentioned above stop being temporary and become chronic. The term employed to describe this process is the General Adaptation Syndrome (G.A.S.) As the body adapts to repeated and constant stress factors, and as chronic symptoms become an accepted part of life, the general level of health declines. Such symptoms include headaches, dizziness, insomnia, blurred vision, swallowing difficulties, aching neck and shoulder muscles, high blood pressure, heart problems, circulatory problems, palpitations, asthma, allergies, indigestion, ulcers, backache, skin rashes, excessive sweating, colitis, sexual problems, depression, phobias, irritability, etc.

Disturbances occur in the blood-sugar equilibrium, giving rise to wild swings in energy levels and mood. If this is accompanied by the excessive use of sugar in the diet, and of stimulants such as tea, coffee and chocolate, the body's ability to maintain a normal blood-sugar level can be severely damaged. (Some researchers see this as a major cause of diabetes.) There is often a tendency to under-perform; self-doubt and insecurity become apparent, and there is a tendency for the defence mechanism to break down, making allergies and infections more likely. Personal relationships become strained, libido often disappears and, as a result of all these changes, further anxiety and stress are created. A vicious circle of declining health, resulting from stress, is the bleak picture which is all too familiar in modern society. Accompanied, as it often is, by poor nutrition, lack of exercise, and debilitating habits such as alcohol, tea, coffee, consumption and cigarette smoking, the formula for disaster is well underway. There is no way in which treatment of any such condition, by the use of drugs and medication, can alter anything but the superficial symptoms. Indeed by doing so and neglecting the underlying causes, symptomatic treatment can do nothing but further harm. Masking and disguising a problem will never provide an answer to it.

This adaptation stage is critical in as much as most, if not all, of the symptoms are still reversible if the underlying stress factors are dealt with and attention is paid to nutrition, exercise, structural integrity, etc. How long this stage lasts depends upon many variables, including inherited factors, as well as the degree of stress, basic health habits, and the degree of emotional support available. After a period of years (ten, twenty or more), depending on this and other variables, the exhaustion stage of the G.A.S. will be reached. At this time, the body simply ceases to be able to cope, and there is a collapse into one or other disease state. Break-down finally occurs when even minor stress factors are not dealt with satisfactorily. At this point there may be collapse into a catastrophic illness, such as coronary heart disease, cancer, etc.

Knowledge of the signs and symptoms of stress, and of some of the ways in which the body copes with stress, can be seen as a necessary step towards understanding the enemy. Without being able to recognize and become aware of stress, it is possible to delude oneself that 'it just won't happen to me'.

The combination of prolonged stress and chronic fatigue has been put forward by some researchers, (Drs Poteliakhof and Carruthers in their report, *Real Health: the Ill Effects of Stress and their Prevention*), as a major factor in the cause of such conditions as rheumatoid arthritis, asthma and hypertension. The combination of lack of sleep, persistent overwork and chronic anxiety is thought to result in hormonal imbalance, notably adrenal exhaustion or sluggishness. This is thought to interact with constitutional and inherited factors to determine the type of disease which develops.

In the field of heart disease, research at Charing Cross Hospital by Dr Peter Nixon (detailed in *Stress and Relaxation* by Jane Madders, published by Martin Dunitz) has shown contributory causes to be sustained and inappropriately high levels of arousal. This is mainly, he suggests, the result of the following factors:

1. pressures exerted by people from whom there is no escape; 2. unacceptable time pressures, deadlines, etc; 3. sleep deprivation, and 4. a high score in the life-style changes list (see page 15).

Dr Nixon states that drugs are unsatisfactory in the treatment of hypertension, since the underlying causes are not dealt with.

Among other stress-induced conditions are those that mimic more serious conditions. 'Symptoms suggesting serious neurological disease are common in patients suffering from anxiety states, or depressive illness, partly, or wholly, attributable to the effects of stress', states Dr Richard Godwin Austin, consultant neurologist of Nottingham General Hospital. 'The most common example seen in the neurological out-patient clinic is the patient suffering from recent onset headaches . . . Patients under physical or psychological stress, frequently develop tension headaches. These may occur in the setting of a depressive reaction, with symptoms of agitation or phobia. The headache often fails to respond to any form of simple analgesic.'

There has also been a good deal of research into stress and its relation to the onset of cancer. The German researcher Dr W. Herberger has noted that chronic anger, disappointment, fear and inability to cope with misfortune often play a role in its development. It has been found that the majority of cancer sufferers have a tendency to dwell on past misfortunes, real or imagined, and they have little sense of the future. Dr Hans

Moolenburg, a noted Dutch physician, has described cancer patients as people who have been 'battered by fate'. It has also been noted that in the U.K., where six out of ten members of the general public acknowledge some belief in God or some spiritual agency, that nine out of ten cancer patients had no such belief. Cancer might therefore be described as, in part, a disease of 'spiritual deficiency'.

Carl Simonton M. D. is one of the world's leading researchers into the effect of the mind on the development of and recovery from cancer. He stated[1]: 'To summarize what I consider the salient points from the literature and my own experience in working in these areas for four years now, the biggest single factor that I can find as predisposing factor to the actual development of the disease is the loss of a serious love object, occuring six to eighteen months prior to the diagnosis. This is well documented in several long-term studies. Now, the significant thing about this is that obviously not everyone who undergoes a serious loss, such as loss of a spouse or a child, develops a malignancy or any other serious disease. That's only one factor. The loss, whether real or imagined, has to be very significant; and even more important is the feeling that it engenders in the patient. The loss has to be such, and the response to the loss such, that it engenders the feeling of helplessness and hopelessness. Therefore, it's more than a loss – it's the culmination of the life-history pattern of the patient. And this also is well defined in the literature.

Personality of the Cancer Patient
'I believe the work that has come out in *Type-A Behaviour and Your Heart* (Friedman and Rosenman, 1975), shows clearly that there is a life-history pattern in the development of heart disease, and I believe that, if we continue to look, we will find predisposing psychological factors in the development of all diseases. Those predisposing factors most agreed upon as (negative) personality characteristics of the cancer patient are:

1. a great tendency to hold resentment and a marked inability to forgive.

---

[1]'Belief Systems and Management of the Emotional Aspects of Malignancy' *Holistic Health Handbook,* 1978.

2. a tendency toward self-pity;
3. a poor ability to develop and maintain meaningful, long-
    term relationships;
4. a very poor self-image.'

As we shall see in the final chapter on the healing power of the mind, an enormous amount of help to cancer patients has been derived by the simple measure of deep relaxation and positive mental imagery. Stress is undoubtedly a major factor in much chronic and acute illness and, if this is so, then any intelligent individual should be able to work out that reversing the stressful input will help considerably towards restoring health. Even more obvious is the fact that by becoming aware of these facts, and by reducing and eliminating stress factors, together with a general stress-proofing programme, prevention of ill health will be greatly enhanced.

There is a school of thought which holds that the attitude and psychological patterns of the individual will determine what patterns disease takes. Examples of this work taken from 'Specific Relations of Attitude to Psychological Change' by P. T. and F. K. Graham, University of Wisconsin Medical School, 1961, are as follows:

Symptom	Attitude
Nausea and vomiting	This person feels something wrong has happened and probably feels responsible. He wishes it had not happened, is sorry it happened, and wishes he could undo it. He wishes things were the way they were before. He wishes he had not done it.
Psoriasis	This person feels something constantly gnawing at him and that he has to put up with it.
Asthma	This person feels left out in the cold and wants to shut the person or situation out. He feels unloved, rejected, disapproved of, shut out,

and he wishes not to deal with the person or situation. He wishes to blot it, or him, out and not to have anything to do with it or him.

Eczema — This person feels he is being frustrated and can do nothing about it. He feels interfered with, blocked, prevented from doing something; he feels unable to make himself understood.

Constipation — This person feels he is in a situation from which nothing could come, but keeps on with it grimly. He feels things will never get any better but has to stick with it.

Migraine — This person feels something has to be achieved and relaxes after the effort. He has to accomplish something, is driving himself, striving. He has to get things done. A goal has to be reached, then he lets down and stops driving himself.

Rheumatoid arthritis — This person feels tied down and wants to get free. He feels restrained, restricted, confined, and wants to be able to move around.

Diarrhoea — This person sees himself faced with a meaningful task and wishes it were over or done with. He wishes impending events were behind him.

(The full list is to be found in *Health for the Whole Person*, Westview Press, Boulder Co., 1981.)

There is another dimension to the way in which stress influences health, to be found in the research conducted over the past 40 years by Prof. Irvin Korr, into dysfunction of spinal regions as part of the 'organizer' of the processes of disease. Stress of a psychological or emotional nature can produce marked changes in the musculoskeletal system, profoundly influencing the overall functioning of the body. All emotional changes are mirrored in the soft tissues. Attitudes such as anger or fear, as well as moods such as excitement or depression, produce muscular postures and patterns. There is also a close link between habitual posture and psychological attitudes and states.

Many postures and defensive tensions arise from anxiety and stress. If this is continued and repeated, restrictions and alterations will take place in the soft tissues. If unreleased, these become self-perpetuating and the source of pain and further stress. The ability to relax is frequently lost and the consequent drain on nervous energy is marked.

Have you ever focused sunlight through a magnifying glass to obtain a pin-point of heat? If, in this metaphor, stress, in all its myriad forms, is represented by the light of the sun, then the focusing mechanism (the lens) is represented by the nervous system. Attention must be given to both aspects of this phenomenon, the stress factors, and how to avoid or minimize them, the body systems which deal with stress and, in particular, the nervous system, which to a large extent determines how the body will cope with it. No two people react to stress in the same way. Even under identical conditions, reactions and effects will vary. While it is important to know what stress is, and how the body reacts to it in general, attention should also be paid to the individual receiving the stress, the unique characteristics of whom will determine the end result.

Why does one person develop an ulcer, another diabetes and yet another high blood pressure? All these conditions might be the apparent result of similar stress patterns. It is obvious, therefore, that the stress factors do not themselves determine the response of the body. The unique make-up and history of the individual is the determining factor in deciding just what aspect of the body will adapt or react in response to any stimulus or stress. Disease, in the final analysis, is the failure on the part of the body to adapt to or cope with the demands placed upon it by the total environment in which it lives. This includes demands of a stressful nature, whether internally generated or externally applied.

What is it that determines which aspect of the body will break down under prolonged stress? There are inherited tendencies, of course, and these must be borne in mind. As already mentioned, there is another key 'organizer' within the body, to which the osteopathic profession, in particular, pays much attention. This is the nervous system and the role played by the nervous system and spinal dysfunction in affecting the way in which particular patterns of ill health are manifested. Professor Korr has established:

1. That there exists in most people's spines, areas or segments, which are abnormal or aberrant, in one of (at least) three ways. These areas may be hypersensitive to pressure, restricted in mobility (movement) or asymmetrical (out of position). Such changes are common, even in apparently healthy people.

2. These areas are abnormal in the degree of tension or tone that is present in the local soft tissues, and the nerves in such areas respond abnormally to *any* stimulus. Some of the nerve cells which deal with messages of sensation, or which direct automatic function or voluntary function, will as a result, be in a state of chronic over-excitability. In other words, they will react more rapidly and more strongly, and for longer than they should, in response to even a mild stimulus of any sort, (emotional or physical).

3. This state of over-reaction is often manifested in the tissues or organs which these nerve cells supply or control.

These abnormally reacting segments may result from injury or postural stress, or they may result from problems in a particular organ or system (say a diseased gall-bladder), which feeds back 'irritable' messages along the nerves supplying it to the spinal centres where local irritation may become chronic and cause changes in the tone of the local soft tissue. Whether the initial cause is reflex (from the organ to the spinal area) or direct (i.e. biomechanical changes in the spine itself), the result is an over-reacting segment of the nervous system.

Since the nervous system organizes the body's adaptive and protective functions in dealing with all environmental variations and extremes (changes of temperature, increased activity, etc.) as well as its reaction to emotional stress (alarm reaction, etc.), such a state of over-excitability in a particular area has enormous local and distant consequences.

For example, instead of an organ being controlled in a balanced harmonious way, it might be kept in a state of near constant over- (or under-) stimulation because the nerve centres controlling its function are in this condition. Such an area is known as a *facilitated* segment (i.e. it allows easier conduction of nerve impulses and activity). If such an area occurs in the upper spinal region, it might be associated, for example, with heart dysfunction. A definite pattern of spinal lesion has been found in most cases of angina pectoris. If, in a mid-spinal area, then the effect might be on the digestive organs, such as the liver or pancreas etc. Now it must be remembered that although the spinal area is maintaining such over- or under- activity via the nervous system, the problem might have originated in the organ itself for a variety of reasons (infection, toxic state, etc.), and the spinal irritation and consequent 'facilitated state' might, originally, have resulted from this.

If stress is part of the individual's life, then the presence in the spine of such areas, and they are the rule rather than the exception, will cause over-reaction in a chronic manner, and the end result will be that the target organ or system will become abnormal in its function. After a while, if unchecked, this will result in damage and dysfunction of the affected organ, and disturbance of the entire body function. Osteopathic methods enable practitioners to speedily identify such 'facilitated' or legioned segments. Osteopathic manipulation of the spine and soft tissues (e.g. neuromuscular technique) can often normalize these areas, but in chronic cases only limited improvement may be possible.

Whatever the mechanical, physical and psychological involvement, it must now be apparent that stress is more than just a nuisance. In the following chapter, I shall discuss methods of assessing your level of stress and will then begin to examine the process of stress reduction and stress-proofing.

For, if taken in hand, there remains the potential for a return to a real state of health, and with it the chance to live life to the full, rather than simply spiralling downwards into an inevitable physical or mental collapse. How can you recognize to what extent stress is currently affecting your health level and potential? Use the checklists in the next chapter to assess this.

3.
Assessing Your Stress

Before looking at ways in which it is possible to start reducing the degree of stress in your life, it is as well to have an idea as to how much is already present and active. It is necessary to assess both the current level of short-term anxiety (if any), and any amounts of underlying anxiety that there might be. The first will give clues as to which factors in your attitudes and everyday life may need adjusting, and the second will give indications of the possible need for professional guidance and counselling. It is also helpful to look at a compendium of signs and symptoms to try to establish clearly just what stress is doing at this moment. Reference to the 'Changes in Lifestyle' list on page 15 can give a guide to the current level of stress to which you are exposed. Remember that a high score on this list indicates a high risk of illness, the actual determining factor is, however, yourself. In this regard, the potential for stress affecting you will be greater if you are already in a high state of arousal engendered by particular personality traits. A further series of predisposing factors are present in the nutritional pattern, daily habits, exercise, etc. and this will also, to some extent, be assessable by means of answering some of the following check-lists.

There are no absolute right and wrong answers in most of these lists. What is being sought is recognition of where you are *now* in relation to stress, and in relation to your own unique potential for achieving optimum high-level health. By following the advice given in later chapters, there is a virtual certainty that, in rechecking in, say, six months' time, a much rosier picture would emerge.

1. *Is stress currently affecting you physically?*
Tick 'yes' ($\checkmark$) if the answer applies more than once weekly. If monthly, answer 'sometimes' ($\pm$), and if less frequently than monthly, answer 'no' (x).

	$\checkmark$	$\pm$	x
Is your sleep disturbed by any of the following:			

(a) difficulty in getting to sleep?
(b) waking frequently in the night?
(c) waking in the early hours, unable to sleep again?

Are you experiencing sexual difficulties? (impotence, lack of desire for sex, etc.)

Do you have difficulty in sitting still without fidgeting?

Do you have headaches?

Do you bite your nails?

Do you feel unusually tired?

Do you have frequent indigestion such as heartburn?

Do you crave for food other than at mealtimes?

Do you have no appetite at mealtimes?

Is bowel function erratic – sometimes constipated, sometimes very loose?

Do you sweat for no obvious reason?

Do you have any 'tics' such as touching the face, hair, moustache, etc. repeatedly?

Do you frequently feel nauseous?

Do you ever faint or have dizzy spells without obvious cause?

Do you feel breathless and tight-chested when not exerting yourself?

Do you cry or feel the desire to cry?

Are you suffering from high blood pressure?

Do you feel obliged to take a drink to 'unwind'?

Do you smoke to calm your nerves?

If you answer 'yes' to two or more of these questions (two 'sometimes' answers are equal to one 'yes') then, almost certainly, your body is adapting to stress, and it is time to take appropriate action. In the absence of organic disease, all such symptoms are remediable by the measures outlined in the following chapters.

Note: Some of the above symptoms can arise from other (e.g. nutritional) causes, but usually these are combined with stress factors.

2. *Is stress currently affecting you mentally?*

                                           ✓   ±   x

Do you lack interest in life?

Do you feel helpless and unable to cope?

Are you irritable without obvious cause?

Are you frequently aware of being afraid of disease?

Do you feel yourself to be a failure?

Do you dislike yourself?

Do you find making up your mind difficult?

Are you disinterested in other people?

Is it difficult to show your true feelings?

Do you feel suppressed (i.e. unexpressed) anger?

Do you feel your appearance has altered for the worse?

Is it difficult to relax and laugh?

Do you feel yourself a victim of other people's dislike or animosity?

Do you feel you are neglected, or have been let down?

Do you feel you have 'failed' in your role as parent, spouse, child?

Do you have a fear of what the future holds?

Do you feel no one understands you?

Do you feel isolated and that there is no one to turn to?

Do you find it difficult to concentrate?

Do you find it difficult to complete one job properly before rushing on to the next?

Do you fear enclosed or open spaces?

Do you feel uncomfortable in touching and being touched?

If you answer 'yes' to three or more of these questions (two 'sometimes' answers equal one 'yes'), then you probably are emotionally affected by stress and action should be taken as outlined in the following chapters. See these signs as a warning and a challenge to be met by personal effort. If on this and the previous list, a combined total of five or more 'yes' answers were given, then it might be advisable to seek professional advice as well as undertaking the health-building, stress-reducing and stress-proofing programmes.

Anxiety Tendency Check-list

You may have had low scores on the previous check-lists, and yet have a tendency towards future problems. Dr Charles Spielberger, Professor of Psychology at the University of South Florida, has given the following shortened anxiety 'trait' self-evaluation scale:

'Read each statement and then circle the appropriate number that indicates how you generally feel. There are no right or wrong answers. Do not spend too much time on any one statement, but give the answer which seems to describe how you generally feel. Add up the eight numbers you have circled to obtain your score.

	Almost never	Some-times	Often	Almost always
I feel nervous and restless	1	2	3	4
I feel satisfied with myself	4	3	2	1
I feel that difficulties are piling up so that I cannot overcome them	1	2	3	4
I feel a failure	1	2	3	4
I have disturbing thoughts	1	2	3	4
I lack self-confidence	1	2	3	4
I feel secure	4	3	2	1
I worry too much over something that really does not matter	1	2	3	4

Only five per cent of the population has a score of ten or

less. Half the population has a score of around fifteen. Only five per cent of the population has a score of over twenty.'

This gives you a guide as to whether your current attitudes are conducive to a stressful future. The advice and exercises given in subsequent chapters should enable you to drastically reduce your score if you carry them out diligently for some months. This, and the previous tests, can become the yardsticks by which you measure the success of your self-help programme.

Type A and B Personality Check-list

Drs Meyer Friedman and Ray Rosenmann have found that certain personality types are more prone to coronary heart disease, and that it is possible for these types to modify their behaviour, and by doing so to reduce their tendency to such disease.

Type A people are three times more prone to heart attacks than Type B. If half or more of the Type A characteristics apply to you, then you belong to this category and should seriously consider modifying your behaviour patterns and life-style. Even three or four Type A characteristics would indicate some inherent stress, and should be modified.

Type A	*Type B*
Very competitive	Not competitive (at work or play)
Strong, forceful personality	Easy-going or retiring
Does things quickly	Methodical or slow in doing things
Strives for promotion at work, or social advancement	Content with present position at work or socially
Wants public recognition	No desire for public recognition
Angered easily by events and people	Slow to anger
Restless when not active	Enjoys periods of idleness
Speaks rapidly	Speaks slowly
Seems to thrive on doing more than one thing at a time	Happiest doing one thing at a time
Walks, gesticulates and eats quickly	Walks, gesticulates and eats without rushing
Impatient at any delay	Patient and not upset by delay

Very conscious of time; enjoys having deadlines to meet	Not time-conscious; ignores deadlines
Always arrives on time	Often late
Taut facial muscles and often clenches fists	Relaxed facial muscles and does not clench fists

Modification is achieved by selecting a particular characteristic and deliberately trying to copy the opposite, Type B, characteristic. For example, the quick eater should allow more time to eat and chew more slowly, until this has become habitual. One by one, all Type A activities can be reduced, or even totally altered.

Nutritional Check-list

The aim of this is to assess whether or not you have an adequate sense of what is and what is not desirable with regard to nutrition. Guidelines as to what constitutes an 'anti-stress' diet will be given in the next chapter.

In the meantime, check your rating by ticking 'yes' ($\checkmark$) for daily, 'sometimes' (±) for no more than once a week, and 'no' (x) for less than once a week.

                                                    $\checkmark$ ±   x

Do you eat refined (i.e. white) flour products?

Do you include sugar (any colour) in your diet?

Do you drink tea, coffee, chocolate or cola drinks?

Do you drink alcohol, other than the equivalent of 1½ glasses wine or 1 pint of beer daily?

Do you eat foods containing any chemical additives (colouring, flavouring, etc.)?

Do you skip meals?

Do you pick at food between meals?

Do you eat more than 6 oz (175g) of animal protein daily?

Do you eat convenience, ready-made (junk) foods e.g. instant mashed potato, T.V. dinners, or tinned foods?

Do you add salt to your food?

Do you eat fried or highly seasoned and spiced foods?

Do you eat fatty meats, smoked or preserved
   foods?
Do you eat fresh fruit?
Do you eat salad?
Do you insist on fresh vegetables only?
Do you use herbs for flavouring food?
Do you ensure adequate fibre in your diet?
Do you eat whole cereal products (such as brown
   rice and wholemeal bread)?
Do you drink herb teas?
Do you take a multivitamin or multimineral
   supplement?
Do you eat non-animal proteins such as seeds,
   nuts, pulses?
Do you eat breakfast?
Do you eat natural yogurt?
Do you believe that what you eat affects your
   health in a major way for good or ill?

   The first twelve questions should be answered 'no' (x). The
second twelve should be answered 'yes' (✓) or 'sometimes'
(±). Modified eating, to the pattern that would provide these
answers, would dramatically alter the ability of the body to
cope with stress and to operate at a higher level of well-being.

Deficiency Check-list
To assess whether or not you are deficient in particular
nutritional substances, check the following signs:

Are your nails ridged?
Do your nails break easily?
Do you have white flecks in your nails?
Do your gums bleed when you clean your teeth?
Do you get frequent mouth ulcers?
Do you have stretch marks in your skin?
Do you get cracks in the corners of your mouth?
Does strong light irritate you?
Are your eyes, mouth or nose dry?
Have you lost your sense of taste or smell?
Do you get cramp?

Does your skin scale or flake?
Do you have a strong body odour?
Do your feet smell strongly?
Do you bruise easily?
Do you recall your dreams on waking?

All of these *might* result from nutritional deficiencies – there could be other reasons of course. If you have a number of positive answers, then you are probably suffering from clinical deficiency in one or more substances. It is worth noting that all nutritional substances (vitamins, minerals, enzymes, trace elements, etc.) are required by the body for optimum function. Any deficiency will have effects on all body systems and functions.

Life-style and Exercise Check-list
Advice regarding this aspect of health maintenance and stress reduction will be found in the following chapters. This check-list is to be used as a means of increasing awareness as to desirable and undesirable habitual patterns in everyday life.

	✓	±	x
Do you work more than 5½ days weekly?			
Do you work more than 10 hours on a work day?			
Do you take less than half an hour for each main meal?			
Do you eat quickly and not chew thoroughly?			
Do you smoke?			
Do you get less than seven hours sleep daily?			
Do you listen to relaxing music?			
Do you practice daily relaxation or meditation?			
Do you take 30 minutes exercise at least three times weekly?			
Do you have a creative hobby (gardening, painting, needlework, etc.)?			
Do you play any non-competitive sport (walking, swimming, cycling), or belong to a yoga or exercise class?			
Do you try to have a siesta or short rest period during the day?			

Do you have regular massage or osteopathic
  attention?
Do you spend at least half an hour outdoors in
  daylight each day?

The first six answers should be 'no'; all 'yes' answers here
show a need for modification. The answers to the following
questions should be 'yes'; all 'no' answers show a need for
modification.

The changes and suggestions made in the next chapter are
designed to modify negative habits and behaviour patterns as
well as improving the entire functional ability of the body to
cope with stress. As has been indicated in earlier chapters,
some such changes require a firm attempt to alter entrenched
attitudes. The check-lists will have shown some of the ways in
which the reader is going to have to act to reach the desired
aim, i.e. nutritional reform and increased attention to exercise.
The more comprehensively these ideas are pursued, the
quicker and more dramatic will be the improvement in health,
ability to function and, in consequence, stress reduction.

In subsequent chapters, methods of relaxation and meditation will be presented, which, when added to the other
modifications, will indeed revolutionize the mind and body.
Positive health is rare today, and this is the ultimate aim of us
all, since through a healthy body we have the opportunity to
achieve the ultimate human desire, which is to be happy.

How would you recognize stress-free, good health? One set
of characteristics could include: sleeping soundly, waking
refreshed; having a good appetite and boundless energy;
having no obvious health problems, or pains; being clear-
minded and able to concentrate; enjoying a mutually satisfying
emotional relationship; enjoying life, with an optimistic
attitude towards the future. Most people, I believe, would
settle for that sort of state – it is certainly worth making an
effort to achieve it.

4.
Starting to Stress-proof Yourself

All of those aspects of the individual's life which are within reasonable control should be examined and, where desirable, adjusted to (a) minimize stress, and (b) raise the level of health and well-being. In this chapter, I will examine the following factors with those two aims in view:

1. Diet and nutrition
2. Exercise
3. Breathing
4. Sleep
5. Environmental factors
6. Life-style
7. Attitudes and beliefs
8. The role of psychotherapy

1. Diet and Nutrition
A well nourished body will function more efficiently than one which is not. A well nourished body will stand up to stress more successfully than one which is not. The majority of people in industrialized countries are not well nourished. Indeed, evidence is growing that, in all social classes, the majority of people are deficient in one or more nutritional elements. A number of surveys conducted in the U.K. and the U.S.A. show clearly that the so-called 'balanced diet', which is supposed to provide all the essential elements of life (protein, minerals, vitamins, etc.), is largely a myth.

In 1980, the Bateman Organization conducted an in-depth survey in the U.K. into people's eating habits. The results showed that only 15 per cent of those interviewed were consuming a diet which could provide even the minimum requirements, as recommended by the D.H.S.S. In the U.S.A. Drs Ringsdorf and Cheraskin have detailed a survey of 860 patients at the Alabama School of Dentistry which showed that around half had possible vitamin C deficiency states, and 6.6 per cent had no vitamin C in the blood at all. A further survey of 120 randomly selected patients at Jersey City Medical Centre showed 88 per cent had a significant deficiency of at least one vitamin, and 63 per cent were deficient in two or more vitamins. Dr Geoffrey Taylor, in an article in the prestigious *Times Health Supplement* in January 1982, stated that '20 per cent of elderly out-patients, 46 per cent of patients with severe chronic disease and 50 per cent of institutionalized elderly people were shown to have levels of vitamin C at which scurvy occurs'.

Amongst the general public, there is an assumption that a normal balanced diet will provide all that the body needs to maintain health. Even if there is some nutritional knowledge (and this is true in only a minority of cases), modern agricultural and commercial practices work against the diet actually containing the nutritional level which it is supposed to. Loss of nutrients starts in the soil, where much land is deficient in trace elements and elements such as zinc, due to the continual heavy use of synthetic fertilizers and over-cropping. Crops are therefore similarly deficient. Further loss of vitamins and minerals occurs between the time of picking and eating, especially where any form of processing is involved. The eating pattern of civilized peoples, with the enormous increase in the consumption of refined carbohydrates and sugars, has deprived the public of complex carbohydrates with their essential nutrients.

High sugar consumption provides many calories, but no nutrients. This can lead to the condition known as hypoglycaemia (low blood sugar), which produces wild swings in mood and behaviour. Characteristic symptoms of this include irritability, fatigue and dizziness. When the blood sugar is low, the individual reacts unpredictably to external stress factors, and is more likely to generate stress emotionally because of unreasonable feelings of edginess.

Industrialized societies create environments in which there is inevitably pollution of water and air, and consequently the absorption by the public of toxic, heavy metals, such as lead, cadmium and aluminium. All these and other factors can result in the individual feeling below par. Irrespective of feelings, any nutritional deficiency makes the body less resistant to stress. One essential nutrient which is frequently lacking in a 'civilized' diet is zinc. Dr Carl Pfeiffer, in his book *Zinc and Other Micronutrients*, states that a deficiency of zinc, among other things, results in behaviour changes and confusion. Under stress, more zinc than usual is excreted with consequent aggravation of such symptoms.

In their book *Psychodietetics*, Drs E. Cheraskin and W. Ringsdorf (Bantam 1976) quote other examples of common deficiencies in relation to stress.

Relatively few people suffer from the most easily diagnosed nutritional ailments. The majority limp through the haze that lies between the daylight of optimal health and the darkness of absolute illness, trying to cope with varying degrees of mental disability.

People don't 'go crazy' suddenly, although they may appear to. Only bones crack from one sharp blow. Prior to an emotional breakdown, chemical imbalances have progressively worsened. The patient has grown increasingly anxious, developed additional physical and emotional symptoms so diversified that they defy a physical diagnosis, but fit nicely into psychiatry's dictionary.

About five per cent of the population suffers from what psychiatrists call anxiety neurosis. Typical symptoms include nervousness, exaggerated fears, sleep disturbances, general pervasive feelings of impending doom, loss of appetite.

Dr John Wozny, a University of Alberta psychiatrist, has found that calcium therapy works wonders for the anxiety-ridden. One of his patients, a thirteen-year old with a long history of emotional complaints, was a bundle of nerves. Tense and friendless, tortured by morbid fears, she particularly dreaded test days at school. Other psychiatrists who treated her had attributed her symptoms to an insecure family atmosphere.

Dr Wozny tested for a nutritional disorder and recommended a high calcium diet. Twenty-three days later, the girl's fears and anxieties were overcome, she was able to get a full night's sleep, and she showed marked improvement at school.

In anxiety neurosis, as in so many other emotional ailments, vitamin deficiencies play an important part. Recent research has uncovered the fact that school children with poor appetites, slow growth rates, and a subnormal sense of taste and smell, are suffering from zinc deficiencies.

Zinc deficiency is more prevalent than supposed. Food refinement and zinc-depleted soils produce zinc-depleted plants, fruits, vegetables, grains, and animals. Dietary zinc supplements and complete mineral or vitamin supplements containing zinc are one answer. Foods from the sea, particularly herring, oysters, and sardines, offer plentiful supplies. Nuts and seeds are also good sources of zinc.

As with zinc, so with magnesium. Deficiencies are no longer rare. Magnesium is vital for nerve conduction, muscular contraction, and the transmission of impulses all along the nervous system. Dr Willard A. Krehl of the University of Iowa, analysing a group of patients with mild magnesium deficiences, found that 22 per cent had convulsions; 44 per cent suffered hallucinations; 78 per cent evidenced mental confusion; 83 per cent were disoriented . . . and 100 per cent startled easily and were alarmed by unexpected movement or noise.

These examples should help us to realize that one factor that is within the individual's control, namely diet, can substantially improve the body's ability to cope with stress, as well as helping towards higher levels of function and well-being. The opposite is also true, of course, and by eating in an imbalanced manner, levels of well-being will be reduced, and the effects of stress are then more likely to be harmful. Poor diet could well be called the 'primary stress factor'.

The following symptoms are common signs of vitamin and/or mineral deficiencies. (There are many others).

Tongue and inner lips are bright red instead of a usual pink colour;
Corners of the mouth are cracked;
Skin scaling at edges of nose;
Nails are ridged, brittle or soft;
Receding gums that bleed easily on brushing;
Changes in texture of skin, such as dryness with a tendency

to crack or flake, especially on thighs and lower abdomen;
Lifeless, thin hair with scurfy tendency;
Swollen inner surface of lower legs and ankles;
Bruising easily;
Low vitality, apathetic and listless;
Slow-healing grazes and cuts;
White flecks in nails;
Poor dream recall;
Tendency to stretch marks on the skin.

The pattern of eating advocated to achieve a balanced diet is as follows: 50 per cent or more of the diet should comprise raw foods such as salad, fruit, seeds, nuts and cereal mixture. One of the main meals should be a salad-based meal with wholemeal bread or a jacket potato and cheese. The other main meal should contain 4-6 oz (100-150g) of protein, either animal or vegetable, and extra vegetables. Desserts should consist of fresh or dried fruit. Snacks should consist of fruit and seeds, (sunflower etc.). Drinks should be taken between meals; either fresh fruit or vegetable juice, spring water, a herb tea, coffee substitute or a yeast-type drink are all suitable alternatives.

Avoid where possible:
All white flour products, such as white bread, cakes, pasta, pastry and biscuits. Replace them with their wholemeal equivalents (available at health food stores);

Avoid where possible:
All white flour products, such as white bread, cakes, pasta, pastry and biscuits. Replace them with their wholemeal equivalents (available at health food stores);
All sugar of any colour and its products such as sweets, jams, soft drinks, ices, etc. Replace these with fruit, dried fruit, sugarless jam, fresh fruit juice, etc;
Polished (white) rice. Replace this with unpolished (brown) rice;
Any foods containing additives, preservatives, colouring, etc. such as most tinned foods;
Tea, coffee and chocolate. Replace these with herb teas,

dandelion or other coffee substitutes (see page 68);
Strong condiments, such as vinegar, pickles, pepper, curry,
    etc. Replace these with herbs;
Alcohol (with the exception of a little wine or real ale);
Margarine;
Salt and salted foods.

Supplements
The following supplements are suggested for any individual
actually suffering from signs and symptoms related to nutritional deficiency or stress. Dosages are arbitrary, and could be
excessive (harmlessly so) for some, but low for others, since it
is known that everyone has individual needs, which vary with
age and factors such as stress.

Vitamin B complex	1 well formulated tablet daily (*Full B with C* or *Stress B*) or 8 Brewer's yeast tablets
Vitamin C	1g daily
Vitamin B^3	(Niacin or nicotinamide) 500mg
Vitamin B^5	(Calcium pantothenate) 500mg daily
Vitamin B^6	(Pyridoxine) 100mg daily
Calcium and magnesium (as Dolomite tablets)	4 daily
Zinc (as Zinc Orotate or B^{13}-zinc)	200mg daily
Potassium (as potassium Orotate or B^{13}-pot.)	150mg daily
Manganese (as Manganese Orotate or B^{13}-mang.)	150mg daily

All should be taken with food.

To understand the reasons for these suggestions, it is
recommended that the following books be read: *Psychodietetics*
by Cheraskin and Ringsdorf (Bantam 1976), *Mental and
Elemental Nutrients* by Dr Carl Pfeiffer (Keats 1975), and *Brain
Allergies* by Drs William H. Philpott and Dwight K. Kalita
(Keats 1980).

2. Exercise
Regular physical exercise is essential for optimum health. The
physiological processes of the body (circulation, respiration,
etc.) will improve in function only if exposed to controlled

exercise; lack of this results in inevitable, slow, but progressive deterioration. In order to cope with the physical and emotional stresses of life, physical fitness is obviously an advantage. It is probably undesirable for highly stressed individuals to participate in competitive sport, since additional stresses frequently occur through competition itself.

Symmetrical forms of exercise, which employ all or most of the body musculature, are the most beneficial. This would include walking, running (jogging), skipping, swimming, cycling or rowing. There is a well known physiological response to vigorous exercise. The body was designed for activity, and the old saying 'what you don't use you lose', may well be applied to muscular strength and functional ability.

In relation to stress, in particular, it has been noted that the hormone, epinephrine (adrenalin) is produced in large quantities, after only ten minutes of sustained activity. This hormone is linked with a general feeling of happiness. Also, as the circulation is rapidly stimulated by exercise, it reduces the presence of lactic acid which results from shallow breathing and inactivity. Lactic acid can induce feelings of fatigue in muscles and is responsible for dulling the brain's activity. The effect of exercise on the system as a whole activates the hormone-producing endocrine glands, stimulates the vital organs, and has a definite, positive effect on lethargic, bored and depressed states of mind.

There is a great advantage in reducing muscular contraction and tension, which may often result from emotional stress, but which may also be caused by lack of exercise, poor posture and habitual working positions. Such muscular tension feeds back impulses, via the nervous system, and creates a degree of central nervous system activity, which prevents the individual from relaxing mentally. In other words, just as mental states can create physical (in this case muscular) tension, so can a prolonged degree of muscular tension influence the emotional and mental state. Physical exercise (as well as relaxation techniques and deep massage or manipulation of the soft tissues) can reduce such tension in the muscles.

There is also the sense of well-being that derives from the release of muscular tension and improved circulatory and respiratory functions. Advice should be sought concerning your individual needs in terms of exercise if you have any health problems. However, as a general guide, *Aerobics* by Dr Kenneth Cooper should be read. This book explains the whole background to this essential part of stress reduction and health promotion. In general terms, unless there are medical contra-indications, everyone should have twenty minutes of active exercise, four times weekly. It is desirable that the pulse rate is monitored in order to achieve the optimum effect, and not to overstrain the physiological processes. An estimate can easily be made as to the optimum pulse rate that should be achieved and maintained during exercise. If the rate achieved is lower than this level, the exercising will be having less than its maximum effect. If the rate goes higher, there exists a risk of strain to the heart. Estimation of the desirable pulse rate is carried out as follows:

From 220, deduct your age. Calculate three-quarters of this figure; this is the target to aim for.

Age 40:   220 - 40   =   180
             ¾ of 180   =   135

A pulse rate of 135 should not be exceeded during exercise by a 40-year-old, but this level should be reached. Progressively, it will be found that more exercise will be required (in terms of effort, etc.) in order to reach this level. This shows that fitness is being achieved.

Many researchers have reported that a physically conditioned person performs tasks such as aptitude tests with better results than before undertaking such a course of physical exercise. It doesn't seem to matter whether the predisposing factors towards negative health factors are physical or psychological, a healthier response is likely to be achieved from a mind in a healthy and fit body. The essential aspect of exercise, in a stress-reducing programme, is that it should be co-ordinated to the individual's needs. This is where Dr Cooper has made such an important contribution, by producing a workable definition of physical fitness, linked to a workable way of measuring the various forms of exercise in relation to the age and present fitness of the individual. An example of the detailed manner in which 'aerobics' graduates the degree of exercise required, is as follows:

Males aged between 20-49 score a 'good' for covering 1.5

miles in 12 minutes (running). If they run 1.65 miles, this is excellent. Walking 4-5 miles at between 15-20 minutes a mile, is the equivalent of this, as is swimming 950 yards in 2.5 to 3.2 minutes per 100 yards or cycling 9 miles at between 4 and 6 minutes per mile. Five such performances weekly are said to maintain good physical condition.

This example shows the usefulness of following Cooper's programme for a variety of exercise with which to produce tangible and desirable targets. Apart from the effects concerning stress and general health, such regular physical exercise has, of course, dramatic effects on heart and circulatory function, which is what it was originally designed for. Can exercise really influence stress and emotion? The following extract from *Health For the Whole Person*, by Drs Hasting, Fadiman and Gordon (Westview Press), gives some indication of the possible value.

The anecdotal evidence includes claims in books and in the popular press by varied authorities that fitness routines enable people to do more work, to feel and look better, to feel more spontaneity and joy in life, and to minimise their high risk behaviours. Psychiatrists and other mental health professionals, committed to various physical disciplines, also claim that regular participation lessens depression, improves self-image, diminishes hypochondriacal behaviours, and mitigates muscle tensions and anxieties.

Dr Kenneth Cooper claims that observations at his Aerobics Centre in Dallas, and elsewhere, support his view that physically fit people are also psychologically fit. Although he steers clear of a cause and effect explanation, Dr Robert Brown at the University of Virginia states that neither he nor his colleagues have ever treated a physically fit, depressed person.

Thaddeus Kostrubala (1977), a psychiatrist and the author of *The Joy of Running* (Pocket Books, New York, 1977), goes farther than most. He claims that running can – in some cases – cure mental illness. In an article by the same title that appeared in *Runners' World* (January 1978), Kostrubala is quoted as suggesting a running regimen for patients diagnosed as schizophrenic. The article cites two studies. The first study at the University of

Missouri involved 100 teachers who participated in swimming, weight-lifting, cycling and jogging. It indicated that all those who evidenced emotional depression in testing before the six-week programme showed an improved state of mind at the end of the experimental period. The second study conducted with prisoners and police officers in training under the direction of Dr William P. Morgan of the University of Wisconsin yielded similar results.

Practitioners of fitness disciplines have also reported states of extreme calm or centeredness, oneness with the universe, and transcendence. This is often the case with marathon or distance runners, but it also occurs with T'ai-chi, swimming and other disciplines (Murphy and White, 1978). Until these studies are replicated with appropriate controls, we can only speculate about their implications. In any event, those mental health professionals who also pursue fitness regimens and attempt to integrate the physical disciplines in their work with patients and clients, do not hesitate to mention that Freud was a great walker and that Jung practised yoga exercises to counterbalance a preoccupation with the intellectual side of life.

Vigorous physical exercise both works off the effects of stress and helps to limit it. A daily session of 20-30 minutes following 'aerobic' guidelines, or as little as four sessions of half an hour each weekly, will transform the level of mental health and produce a sense of well-being more dramatically than words can describe.

It is also desirable to include in the stress-proofing programme, one or other of a slow, stretching-type exercise, such as yoga or T'ai-chi. Initially, the more vigorous exercises are more important. Once these are established in the daily routine, lessons in yoga or T'ai-chi should be undertaken. This will greatly enhance balance, relaxation and mind-body harmony.

3. Breathing
The individual's level of tension is reflected in his pattern of breathing. When relaxed and contented, breathing is slow and rhythmic, and although not necessarily deep, it should involve some movement of the entire rib cage and movement of the diaphragm. When tense, breathing is rapid and shallow.

Usually only the upper part of the chest will move, and the lower lungs remain virtually unused, with relatively little diaphragmatic movement. Many relaxation and meditation methods incorporate breathing into their programme, some as a major, and others as only a minor or introductory element. Some understanding of the respiratory mechanism is therefore desirable.

The diaphragm is a large, dome-shaped muscle, which forms the boundary between the abdominal cavity and the thoracic cavity. On breathing in, the diaphragm should contract and descend, thus producing a partial vacuum in the chest cavity which is filled by the expanding lungs as air rushes into them. During the breathing out phase, the diaphragm relaxes back, upwards, into its domed position. This encourages the expulsion of 'used' air from the lungs. Breathing in is further augmented by the expansion of the ribs, aided by the muscle groups that control them, just as efficient exhalation is enhanced by the rib cage contracting. Chronic dysfunction and restriction of the diaphragm and the muscles associated with breathing, may result from a variety of causes including injury, bad posture and emotional stress. Poor breathing patterns are the rule rather than the exception in 'civilized' man.

Breathing is the one vital function over which we can exercise voluntary (i.e. conscious) control. Its intimate connection with our emotions allows us an opportunity to influence the effects of stress and tension for the better by learning how to introduce a correct, natural, full breathing pattern at will.

The following breathing exercises are not specifically relaxation exercises but may be used as or 'separately from' the relaxation and meditation methods which, hopefully, you will select from those presented and will then practice twice daily. The objective in these breathing exercises is to learn how to breathe fully, so that in stressful situations or environments, you will be able to, inobtrusively, introduce one or other of them, and overcome the tendency for shallow, tension-inducing breathing. They can be practised when standing, walking or at rest. They often assist in inducing sleep in the insomniac. Before learning the exercises, however, one should be aware of the phenomenon of 'over-breathing'. In many people under stress, there exists a tendency to sigh, catch the breath, gasp and generally to introduce 'laboured', heavy breathing. In a crisis, this might well be an appropriate response (see the section on the 'fight and flight' reaction in Chapter 2), but in the aftermath of a crisis it is not appropriate. Unfortunately for many, they seem unable to return to a normal pattern of breathing and continue to hyperventilate. Although it may seem harmless to increase the availability of oxygen in this way, it is really this and the over-exhaling of carbon dioxide which can produce such short-lived symptoms as dizziness, tingling and numbness of the hands and scalp, vital disturbances, etc. It is useful, in all breathing exercises, to concentrate most on the exhalation phase. If this is adequate, then the quality of the breathing in that follows will be greatly improved.

Three-stage Breathing
Practise this lying down on your back. If the lower-back cannot comfortably touch the floor, then either bend the knees, or place a cushion under them.

1. Rest your hands on the upper part of the chest and breathe in slowly, so that this part of the chest rises slightly. Exhale and ensure that all air has been expelled before allowing the inrush of fresh oxygenated air to again expand this part of the chest. Repeat five to ten times. The hands are passive, just resting on the chest and sensing the rhythmic rising and falling of the upper chest cage.

2. Place the hands on the lower ribs just to each side of the breastbone (sternum), so that the fingertips almost touch on exhalation. As you inhale, feel the ribs expand outwards and away from the body, taking the hands apart from each other. Concentrate on the exhalation being complete, so that the finger-tips come, once again, towards each other and the ribs crowd in towards the centre of the body. The next inhalation again produces the sideways expansion of the rib cage as the air fills the lungs. Repeat this five to ten times.

3. Rest your hands on your abdomen at the level of the navel.

Inhalation should now commence with the abdomen expanding outwards to allow the downward excursion of the diaphragm and the filling of the lower lobes of the lungs. As this happens, the hands will be felt to be pushed upwards (towards the ceiling). Exhalation reverses this, and as the diaphragm returns to its high, domed position, the abdomen flattens and the hands return to their starting position. Repeat this five to ten times.

That completes the three individual stages of breathing. The order is not vital, but after practising these three stages for some days, they should be combined into the complete breathing exercise as outlined below. The speed of these exercises should be slow – they should never be hurried. If ten cycles of each stage are peformed, this would take, at most, four minutes – so there must be time to do them, even in the busiest day!

Complete Breathing Cycle
This should accompany the performance of the individual stages (above) once you feel satisfied with your ability to do them as described. It can be used on its own as a means of reducing arousal or tension at any time.

Caution: after any deep-breathing exercise, rest for a minute or two with the breathing in a natural, uncontrolled pattern, and then rise first to sitting and then to a standing position slowly. It is not uncommon to feel a little light-headed for a few minutes following the full performance of all the stages of breathing. Simply doing a complete breathing cycle a few times will not produce this effect though.

Lie on the floor as above. Place your hands where they feel most comfortable. Breathe out completely and then start the complete breath by expanding the abdomen slightly (as in stage three), filling the lower lungs with air before allowing the lateral and upward expansion of the lower ribs to enable that part of the lungs to fill as well. Finally, complete the inhalation by expanding the upper ribs forward to fill the upper lungs and air passages. This slow filling of the whole chest cavity with its maximum capacity of air should take a count of between eight and fifteen seconds, depending upon your capacity and control. There should be no straining or tension during the full breathing cycle. If you feel laboured and tensed during the exercise, then shorten the time.

Exhaling reverses the procedure, with the upper passages emptying first, then the lower ribs collapsing gently back to their resting position, and finally the expanded abdomen deflating, and the 'used' air from the lowest reaches of the lungs being expelled. Try to see the process as a bellows emptying. The last air should be expelled with a slight contraction of the abdominal muscles, to take them just beyond their resting position. Pause, with no air in the lungs, for no more than two or three seconds. The refilling of the lungs, following the same slow pattern, is then almost automatic as the air rushes in to fill the vacuum thus created. Inhalation and exhalation should take the same length of time. Repeat this five to ten times or perform the exercise just once or twice in any appropriate situation.

Note: All breathing should be through the nose.

There are times, especially when under stress of an emotional nature, when this exercise pattern will be more difficult to perform. The whole procedure may be jerky and accompanied by sobs or sighs. This is an excellent reason for continuing. Eventually, there may be an intense desire to laugh or cry. This type of emotional release, which may accompany deep breathing, should not be suppressed. Let it happen, and if possible pay attention to any thoughts or memories that come into the mind when it happens. These can help to give insights into underlying causes of anxiety. If it happens repeatedly, talk to your doctor about it, as counselling or psychotherapy might be a help in resolving the problem.

4. Sleep

One of the most striking symptoms of a stress condition is its disturbance of the normal sleep pattern. This may take the form of great difficulty in getting to sleep, or of waking after an hour or two of sleep and being unable to go off again, or waking after five or six hours, feeling unrefreshed, and unable to sleep again, or of the sleep itself being fitful and broken with a consequent feeling of sluggishness in the morning. The disturbed sleep itself often becomes a source of further stress, as the individual worries about not getting enough sleep, and as the effects of insomnia begin to become apparent. Amongst the results of sleep deprivation are the following: deterioration in perception; slower, more erratic reaction times to stimuli; impairment of general performance; lower energy level; memory lapses; pain sensitivity increase; deterioration of judgement and motivation; impairment of concentration and a tendency towards a negative, irritable and depressed state. In mild cases of insomnia, such changes may be of a slight nature, but nevertheless add to the overall stress level.

Sleep itself should be as natural and simple a part of living as breathing. It is certainly vital to health, and probably to life itself. The quality of life and the capacity to work well and to enjoy life depend upon adequate sleep. The natural rhythms of life that govern our functions are inborn. The cycles of increasing and decreasing activity are continuous within the body system. Sleep is one such a cycle. The normal sleep pattern starts with lying down, with the eyes closed, in a state somewhere between being awake and truly asleep. At this point, the brain wave pattern is called the 'alpha' state. This is the same as the state achieved in deep relaxation or meditation. Dreaming is also possible at this stage. The next stage lasts for between 90 minutes and two hours and takes the form of a very deep, non-dreaming sleep, known as the non-R.E.M. (R.E.M. stands for rapid eye movement) or 'delta' stage. If wakened during this stage, almost nothing of what happens will be recalled, and behaviour will be zombie-like. After this, a gradual change takes place and the R.E.M. stage is reached. Dreaming begins; the closed eyes can be seen to be moving rapidly, and there is often body movement as well.

The significance of dreams as a source of psychological release deserves emphasis. A leading researcher, Dr André Tridon, has stated: 'The real mission of dreams is to free your unconscious, to relieve the tension due to repression and to give absolutely free play to the organic activities which build up'. Most dreaming takes place during the R.E.M. stage, which is that part of sleep most disrupted by sleeping tablets. Dreaming is felt to be important in the consolidation into the memory of new information. Distressing symptoms are seen to result from dreams being constantly disturbed experimentally. Dreams are known to be vital to mental health. Whether any meaning can be divined from remembered dreams is a much debated point.

From this point on (after the dreaming stage), sleep becomes progressively lighter. It is now known that vital hormone production from the pituitary gland occurs during the 'delta' stage, and that this has a restorative and refreshing effect on the body as a whole. In civilized society, natural sleep rhythms are not given much chance to operate. There are a variety of factors which work against the sort of pattern of sleep that nature demands. There is, for instance, a great deal of pressure in modern society towards conformity. Getting up and getting to a place of work or study, or getting up and doing what has to be done in terms of housework, family duties, shopping, etc., all necessitate waking and rising at a time that is determined, not by the needs of the body, but by whatever demands these activities produce. In most industrialized societies, programmes of work or study make no allowance for rest periods during the day, and the result is, all too often, that the individual reaches the end of the working day in an overtired state. If additional stress factors are also part of this picture (difficult journeys to and from the place of work, difficult relationships, financial anxieties, etc.), then the pattern begins to look ominous. With a combination of the above factors taking effect, a variety of changes can occur which are evidenced by sleep disturbances. At this stage, many turn to medication for help. The results are less than satisfactory. The quality of sleep accruing from the use of sleeping tablets is poor. The drugs themselves are often addictive and usually have side-effects and, above all else, they deal (and not too well at that) with the symptoms and ignore the causes of illness, which is bad medicine indeed.

Research has shown that sleeping tablets are largely ineffective, and that among the common side-effects of these drugs are indigestion, respiratory ailments, loss of appetite, skin rashes, increased blood pressure, kidney and liver dysfunction, lowered resistance to infection, mental confusion and memory lapses, circulatory problems, etc. Apart from these side-effects, most of the drugs are addictive, despite the fact that almost all sleeping tablets lose their effectiveness within a few weeks. The fact is that when they do work, they do not induce sleep, but simply knock the individual out and being unconscious is not the same as sleeping. When sleeping tablets are taken, they poison the system. One U.S. Food and Drug Administration report in 1975 (on scopolamine and bromides, two common ingredients of sleeping pills) stated: 'The effective dose differs little from the poisonous dose'. The director of a leading American sleep research laboratory has stated 'All sleeping pills become ineffective after two or three weeks of steady use. After that period of time, they simply don't work.' The greatest irony of all is that, because of their effect on the body, sleeping tablets actually result in worse insomnia after withdrawal. If sleep has become disturbed, then it is well worth considering some of the factors that can contribute towards the normalization of this vital function. From our earliest years, we establish patterns of activities that are performed before going to bed. The type of clothing worn, the type of bed-clothes used, are part of the pattern. Any variation in the pre-sleep ritual can disturb sleep, and it pays to look at the sort of things that were part of the pre-sleep pattern before sleep became a problem. Such things as bathing, putting clothes away, reading, listening to music, praying, the position of the body, and sex, among other things, all play a major part in many people's pre-sleep rituals. If sleep is disturbed, it is often possible to compensate for this by taking a midday nap, either after or instead of a meal. This will not detract from the chance of sleeping well that night, but, by helping to restore a degree of relaxation, will actually enhance it. It is also important to ensure that adequate exercise is being taken, but not just prior to going to bed, unless this is part of the pre-sleep ritual.

Sex, or lack of it, is a major area of stress, and advice from an expert may be necessary if this is the factor producing insomnia. Individual counselling is the ideal, and your medical adviser should be consulted to arrange for this, if needed.

Obvious causes of a change in the sleeping pattern should be identified, and the usual pattern of preparation for sleep maintained in the confidence that the sleep pattern will re-establish itself. There is no cause for panic or anxiety over such changes. If the change is to waking in the early hours, it often helps to get up rather than lie and worry. A great contribution towards a return to normal sleep will be made via relaxation and/or meditation exercises (see Chapters 5, 6 and 7).

Nutrition also plays a part in normalizing disturbed sleep, just as it does in most health problems. A great number of insomniacs have been found to be hypoglycaemic (sufferers of low blood sugar). This is frequently the result of a diet containing too much sugary, starchy food and caffeine-rich beverages such as coffee, tea, cola drinks and chocolate (see page 68), as well as an inadequate quantity of fresh fruit and vegetables. Many researchers have found insomniacs to have low levels of vitamin B_3, B_6, B_{12}, zinc, calcium, magnesium and manganese, all of which indicates an inadequate dietary pattern. The general advice in such cases is to consult a physician who is nutritionally oriented. In the meantime, follow the pattern outlined in the section on nutrition (page 45).

One recent major breakthrough in research indicates that a substance known as L-Tryptophan plays a vital role in normal sleep. It is an amino acid (i.e. one of the building blocks of protein) and is contained in milk, meat, fish, eggs, nuts, soya beans and other protein-rich foods. Taking concentrated tablets of L-Tryptophan has been shown to frequently hasten and prolong sleep in insomniacs, without any side-effects. This amino-acid helps to produce a substance in the body known as serotonin, which appears to be vital to sleep. The diet should of course supply this substance, but for the sleep-disturbed individual, a 1g dose to be taken twenty minutes before going to bed is recommended by a major researcher in this field, Dr E. Hartman of Boston State Hospital. L-Tryptophan is available from health food stores (combined with other sleep-assisting supplements such as calcium and vitamin B_6), as *Somnamin* (manufactured by *Cantassium Co.*, 225 Putney Bridge Road, London SW15).

Sleep is vital and sleep is natural. If it is disturbed, the causes can usually be found in the pattern of life and, by correcting these, it should return to normal. This means eating correctly, ensuring adequate exercise, practising relaxation and/or meditation, sorting out areas of stress (work, relationships, sex, etc.), and letting nature do the rest.

5. Environmental Factors

Ions

Ions are electrically charged molecules present in the atmosphere around us. Some are positively charged, and others negatively. We inhale these ions as we breathe and, to a lesser extent, absorb them through the skin. In fresh air, there are between 1,000 and 2,000 ions per cubic centimetre, but in cities there are frequently fewer than 100 ions per cubic centimeter.

Ions are adversely affected by such factors as atmospheric pollution, dust, smoke, etc. They can be trapped by man-made fibres, air-conditioning, heating units, television screens, etc. It is the negative ions which are mainly affected in this way, and it is in areas of relatively high negative ion concentration that people feel better (i.e. at the seaside, in the mountains). Conversely, people tend to feel lethargic and depressed when they are in an atmosphere heavily charged with positive ions. This would be the case in a centrally heated or smoky room, or just before a thunderstorm or during certain seasonal winds such as France's mistral.

People react differently to ion imbalance. For some, there appears to be only a minor awareness of such variations, for other more susceptible individuals, however, a decrease in negative ionization can result in marked physiological and psychological changes. For example, there may be an increase in the production by the body of such hormones as histamine. This can result in greater tendencies to allergic reactions, as well as sleep-pattern disturbances, headaches and mood changes. Also as a result of ion imbalance, there may be a prolonged release of adrenalin, which can produce any or all of the symptoms associated with stress (see Chapters 3 and 4). It is now possible to restore ion balance by the use of ionizer machines. These relatively inexpensive machines can be a boon in the home or workplace to anyone suffering from these effects of the twentieth century.

Full-spectrum Light

Just as an imbalanced diet may be called malnutrition, so exposure to 'improper' light may result in an adverse health response and may be called 'malillumination'. Light is composed of waves of radiant energy and is measured in wavelengths (the distance between one wave crest and another). Sunlight produces 'white' light, which contains all the wavelengths. As well as all the colours, this also contains infra-red (heat) waves and ultra-violet (UV) waves. The full electromagnetic spectrum of waves is therefore present in sunlight. Artificial light contains practically no ultra-violet waves and ultra-violet light is also blocked by glass windows, spectacles and wind-shields. The spectrum of light reaching our bodies and eyes, is further distorted by skin and sun tan lotions, contact lenses, tinted glasses, etc.

Atmospheric pollution further interferes with the full light spectrum being available to the individual. Research into the consequences of light starvation has shown that it results in potentially dramatic effects on the mind and body. The endocrine system, which produces the hormones of the body, is influenced by light received by photo-receptor cells in the retina of the eye. Acting as transducers, these cells convert light energy into chemical energy and, via neurochemical pathways, this influences the master glands in the brain, the pineal and the pituitary and, via these, the whole body. There are a number of physical and behavioural effects, which have been researched in the U.S.A. by scientists such as Dr Joseph Meites of the University of Michigan and Dr John Ott, who has written widely on the subject. He writes as follows:

The behavioural effects of light were evident in a 1973 study of school children which we undertook in Sarasota, Florida. My experiences with trying to mature plants under fluorescent lights left me with serious misgivings concerning their extreme wavelength distortion and radiation emissions, and the possible effects of this abnormal light 'diet' on human beings. My investigations led to the development of full-spectrum fluorescent lighting, which closely duplicates the natural sunlight outdoors.

The 1973 study, conducted by the Environmental Health and Light Research Institute, involved four first-grade classrooms.

Standard, cool, white fluorescent tubes and fixtures with solid plastic diffusers remained in two of the rooms, full-spectrum fluorescent tubes were installed with lead foil shields to eliminate radiation from the cathodes. A combination aluminium 'egg crate' and wire grid screen replaced the conventional plastic diffusers. In addition to allowing the full-spectrum light to pass through unfiltered, the screens grounded the radio frequency (RF) energy normally given off by all fluorescent tubes. This RF energy is known to cause inaccurate readings from computers and from the sensitive equipment in hospital scanning rooms. A Russian study reports that RF energy from fluorescent tubes has been recorded in electroencephalogram readings of human brain waves.

Time-lapse cameras, concealed in specially built compartments, took random sequences of pictures in the classrooms. The teachers knew of the program, but not when pictures would be taken; the children were not aware they were being photographed.

Under the standard, cold, white fluorescent lighting, some first-graders demonstrated nervous fatigue, irritability, lapses of attention and hyperactive behaviour. They could be observed fidgeting, leaping from their seats, flailing their arms and paying little attention to their teachers.

In the rooms which received full-spectrum lighting, the children's behaviour began to improve markedly within one month after the new lights were installed. Nervousness and excessive activity diminished, and teachers reported improved classroom performance. Many factors undoubtedly contribute to hyperactivity and learning disabilities, but these observations clearly indicate that light and radiation may be influential.

Study of the behavioural effects of artificial illumination is continuing with animal studies at the National Institute for Environmental Health Sciences in Triangle Park, North Carolina, and with a study I am undertaking for the State of Washington penal system, to assess the effects of lighting and colours on prisoner behaviour.

The Sarasota school experiment also included dental examinations of participating children. Those in the rooms with full-spectrum lights showed a significantly lower incidence of cavities, than those in the rooms with standard lights. Often studies with rats and hamsters suggest that the orange, red and infra-red portions of the spectrum (in which the standard, cool, white fluorescent lights are deficient) may influence resistance to caries. I suspect that some body chemicals – possibly hormones – which enhance resistance to caries, may be activated by exposure to these portions of the spectrum.

As yet we do not fully understand the role played by light on the body. However, the examples quoted above by John Ott indicate clearly that general health and behaviour can be dramatically influenced by attention to this aspect of 'nutrition'.

Full-spectrum lighting is available in the U.K. and the U.S.A. It is also advisable to spend at least half an hour outdoors each day with the eyes unshielded by glasses. If this is not possible, being by an open window during daylight will help. Looking at the sun is not to be recommended. Full-spectrum light reaches the retina, even on a cloudy day, as long as its way is not blocked by glass. Just as proper nutrition aids stress-proofing, so do full-spectrum light and a balanced ion environment.

Colour

Research is being actively conducted into the effects on mood, health, etc. of the colours to which we are exposed. Tests (such as the Luscher system), using colour cards, can assess the state of mental harmony and the general stress level. Colour is our visual interpretation of a particular band of electromagnetic radiation. When considering how colour can actually affect us, we are, to a large extent, in the realms of speculation. One theory believes that colour acts on the pineal gland, which certainly reacts to changes in illumination. Another theory is that colour effects chemical changes in human cells by triggering the release of vital substances in the nerve endings. It is now known that axonal transport is a reality and the potential of this finding is enormous. Axonal transport means that nerves do not just relay messages, but actually transport substances (protein, fats, hormones) to the areas they supply, *and* carry substances back towards the higher centres from these areas.

If colour can affect nerve endings and alter the feedback along the nerve, then physiological and psychological change could result from this influence. Other theories are concerned with areas not amenable to scientific investigation at this stage, such as the effect of light on the 'etheric body' or 'aura' of the individual. Kirlian photography has shown that there exists an electromagnetic field around all life forms. Those that claim to see the aura say that its colour varies with the individual's state of health. In practical terms, blue is the colour which induces relaxation and, if possible, this should be used in clothing and decoration in preference to reds and yellows, which are stimulating and tension-inducing. Reference to the visualization of colour will be found in the section on meditation.

6. Life-style – The Common Props

The population of the industrialized world is becoming increasingly dependent upon readily available drugs as aids to 'coping' with modern life. These range from the prescribed tranquillizing drugs and alcohol, tobacco and stimulants such as caffeine, to the use of cannabis, cocaine and heroin. The prescribed use of mood-altering drugs, such as librium and valium continues to escalate enormously. Six out of ten of all prescriptions in the U.S.A. are for one or other of these. They are considered mild, and have anti-anxiety effects. In short-term use, such as the shock experienced after the death of a close relative, these might serve a useful purpose. Long-term use, however, should never be necessary if sufficient attention is paid to the causes of the anxiety. Librium and valium produce effects such as drowsiness, lethargy, unsteady walking, blurred vision, slurred speech, nausea, menstrual irregularity, liver dysfunction, etc. These are, however, much safer than earlier sedatives such as phenobarbital, which blocked nerve transmission. Other sedatives had similar side-effects, as well as often producing severe liver problems and anaemia. All these drugs can produce psychological dependency if used for an extended period.

In both industrialized and under-developed societies there is a remarkable similarity in the effects upon the body in general, and the nervous system in particular, of the substances which are eaten, drunk and smoked. Tobacco is smoked in a variety of ways, and also chewed. Alcohol, derived from an enormous variety of sources, is drunk for its rapid intoxicating qualities. A number of non-alcoholic, but equally effective substances also exist. Tea, coffee, cocoa and cola drinks are consumed for their stimulating effects on the nervous system. The hazards of cigarettes and inhaling tobacco smoke, are so well documented as to need no reiteration. The rise in alcohol consumption and the increase in diseases relating to its consumption are equally well established.

A further common prop is the use of sugar-rich foods to provide a quick 'lift'. Whether rapidly absorbed sugary foods are eaten in order to raise the blood sugar level, or whether tea, coffee, cola, cocoa or tobacco smoke are used to stimulate the production of adrenalin, along with the release of sugar by the liver, the effect is much the same. The tired, edgy individual's system is kicked back into life, much as a whip is used on a tired horse. The effect of this repeated elevation of the blood sugar level is to force the pancreas to constantly neutralize the excess sugar in the blood by producing insulin. It is worth recalling that the blood sugar level will also be increased every time there is a stress-induced reaction, as described in Chapter 3. This sort of fluctuation in the blood sugar level, combined with the strain placed on the adrenal glands and the pancreas, can result in one of several conditions becoming apparent. Should the pancreas fail to respond adequately to the demands made of it, a diabetic state will exist. The blood sugar will be high, and the body will become unable to deal with it. There is evidence, however, that the opposite situation occurs more frequently. This involves an over-production of insulin, which leads to low blood sugar, known as hypo-glycaemia. In such cases, the 'prop' has become a burden and far from helping the stressed individual, it will have added to his problems. This constant swing from a stress-induced 'high', resulting in the over-production of insulin and the consequent 'low', leads, in turn, to a quick lift being sought (through sugar, a stimulant drink or a cigarette), and thus a repeat of the cycle.

Coffee contains caffeine; tea contains caffeine, theophylline and tannin; cola contains caffeine; cocoa (and therefore chocolate) contains caffeine, theobromine and tannin. These substances, caffeine, theophylline and theobromine are drugs, usually referred to as xanthines, which stimulate the nervous system, make the kidneys produce more urine, stimulate the heart muscles and the circulation, etc. The immediate effect is to reduce any feeling of tiredness, and to make for improved muscular effort. Tea contains 50 to 125 mg of caffeine per cup; coffee contains 100 to 150 mg of caffeine per cup; cocoa contains about 50 mg of caffeine per cup, and the average cola drink contains 40 to 55 mg of caffeine.

Reactions to caffeine vary with each individual, but if the daily intake exceeds 1000 mg (say 8-10 cups of strong tea and/or coffee and the odd piece of chocolate or cola drink), the following common side-effects are likely to be experienced: difficulty in sleeping; excitability and restlessness; trembling; palpitations; rapid breathing; ringing in the ears; acid stomach and indigestion; frequency of passing water. Drinking the occasional cup of any of these beverages is unlikely to do any harm, but it should be noted that psychological dependence on caffeine is common, as evidenced by the number of people who do consume such liberal amounts of these socially permitted drugs. There are three distinct signs of addiction which are displayed by consumers of caffeine (or alcohol or tobacco) in any quantity. These are: tolerance of the drug, withdrawal symptoms and craving after deprivation. Many scientific studies confirm that all these substances do have these addictive properties.

Since society is unlikely to rapidly change for the better, it means that there is a clear choice. People must be taught to cope with stress naturally, or the use of addictive props, be they freely available or on prescription only, will continue to rise. (There may, admittedly, be times of crisis when drugs, prescribed and used with care, may be useful). The individual who *knowingly* relies on such drugs will also be prepared to accept the consequences in terms of diminished health levels. The individual who does so in ignorance deserves pity, as well as education about the alternatives. Along with an overall reassessment of the individual's diet, and the application of positive stress-reducing methods, such as meditation and relaxation exercises, the overcoming of dependence upon the common stimulant and sedative drugs will be a major step towards recovery of full health potential. It is suggested that professional help be sought if any difficulty is experienced in modifying such habits. In general, the following guidelines may be of assistance:

Cigarettes: If the individual smokes for stimulation ('it gives me a lift'), then regular exercise can help to reduce this need. If the motivation is one of enjoying the ritual of smoking ('I like the whole procedure and enjoy looking at the smoke'), then alternatives can be found to keep the hands busy (doodling, worry beads, etc.). If the smoker feels the motive is relaxation ('it helps me unwind'), or if smoking is a response to anger or anxiety, then the application of the techniques in this book will help to find a safer alternative. If smoking is pure habit ('I smoke automatically'), then a little serious thought as to the consequence should aid a determined effort to stop. If there is a true addiction ('I yearn for a smoke if deprived for a while'), then very strong motivation will be needed to break the habit. Hypnotism and acupuncture can assist in motivating the individual and in reducing withdrawal symptoms. The introduction of a number of food supplements in the diet will also help. These include:

1. One good vitamin B-complex tablet daily;
2. 100-500mg of vitamin B^3 (nicotinamide) daily;
3. 1g of vitamin C daily;
4. Calcium and magnesium in the form of dolomite tablets – 2-4 daily.

Take all these with food.

Alcohol: At an extremely moderate level, consumption of alcohol has been shown to have a stress-reducing effect. This level is bound to vary with individual characteristics, but it is unlikely to exceed the equivalent of 1½ glasses of wine, ¾ pint of beer, 1 measure of spirits, daily.

Anything in excess of this is almost certain to create more problems than it solves. If difficulty is experienced in keeping consumption to this level, then it may be better to stop altogether.

A number of nutritional aids exist to assist with the withdrawal symptoms experienced by regular consumers of alcohol when they stop or cut down their intake drastically. One of these is an amino acid called L-glutamine. It is suggested that three

500mg tablets be taken daily during the withdrawal stage, together with a high-dosage vitamin B-complex tablet (such as *Strong B*). Both these supplements are marketed by *Cantassium Co.*, 225, Putney Bridge Road, London SW15. In addition, at least 1g of vitamin C and a multi-mineral compound should be taken. It is most important to ensure a balanced, regular dietary pattern.

Tea, coffee, cocoa, chocolate and cola beverages should be cut out of the diet and replaced by herbal teas, coffee substitutes, yeast extract drinks and fruit or vegetable juices. One effect of caffeine-containing foods and drinks is to stimulate the liver to release stored sugar. If the diet also includes quantities of refined sugars, then the body's task of retaining a reasonable blood sugar level is made even more difficult. After each 'injection' of sugar (be it direct from food or via the liver from a stimulant drink), a response is required from the body's sugar-controlling mechanism. This involves insulin production by the pancreas and consequent fluctuations in blood sugar levels, accompanied by mood changes, irritability and greater vulnerability to stress. Refined sugar and carbohydrates such as white flour products, should therefore play little or no part in the 'stress-proofing' diet.

Changing Your Habits
1. Avoid working more than ten hours daily and ensure that you have at least 1½ days a week free of routine work. If at all possible, an annual holiday 'away from it all', should be arranged.

2. During each day, have at least two relaxation or meditation periods. Time should be set aside morning and evening, or just prior to a meal.

3. Perform active physical exercise for at least ten minutes daily, or for 20-minute periods four times each week.

4. Balance the diet and eliminate stress-inducing foods and drinks.

6. Try to move, talk and behave in a relaxed manner.

7. Seek advice about any sexual or emotional problems that

are nagging away at the back of your mind, or which are causing conscious anxiety.

8. If there are actual stress-inducing factors at work or home, which can be altered, then make concrete steps towards these changes.

9. Cultivate a creative rather than a competitive hobby, e.g. painting, DIY, gardening, etc.

10. Try to live in the present, avoiding undue reflection on past events or anticipating possible future ones.

11. Concentrate on whatever the current task is, always finishing one thing before starting another.

12. Avoid making deadlines or 'impossible' promises that could lead to stress. Take on only what you can happily cope with.

13. Learn to express feelings openly in a non-beligerent way and, in turn, learn to listen carefully to other people.

14. Accept personal responsibility for your life and health – don't look outside yourself for causes or cures, apart from the objective guidance and practical advice available from a health professional.

15. Greet, smile at and respond towards people in the same way that you would like to be treated.

16. Introduce negative ionization into the home or work place and ensure adequate exposure to full-spectrum light.

7. Attitudes and Beliefs

In the field of stress there are many factors over which we have no control. We must all experience the life-style changes which are an inevitable part of the process of living, such as growing up, going to school, leaving home, getting work, etc. We are all, at some time or another, subject to sudden stressful events, such as deaths and other personal natural disasters. We are, in the main, also subject to anxiety over such imponderables as world peace, economic recession, etc. Some will cope with these situations well; others will add to this list an array of self-induced stress factors, which are the direct result of (a) not dealing with problems that can be solved, and (b) self-generated stress, brought about by attitudes, beliefs and personality factors, all of which may be revised or modified. Since the objective of this book lies partly in helping the individual to become aware of possible ways to reduce and avoid stress, some attention must be paid to these self-generated aspects of the problem (attitudes and beliefs).

Uncertainty is a major cause of stress, and practical steps need to be taken to reduce this factor. For example, if there is a threat of redundancy, all alternative sources of work should be methodically explored. Re-training should be considered. Updating skills to improve future employment opportunities should be considered. If already out of work, it is vital that the individual maintains the skills and knowledge he has acquired. Mind and body should be kept active and a positive attitude must be cultivated. The alternative is to fret and become edgy and sleepless, thus reducing the chances of gaining the desired objective, due to declining personal efficiency, brought about by stress.

Similar action is possible in most cases of uncertainty. For example, an unexplained symptom can often trigger the imagination to dream up all kinds of sinister implications. Once a diagnosis is arrived at, a positive course of action can be undertaken and, although there may still be some anxiety as to the outcome, the main source of uncertainty and stress is dispelled. Individuals can always cope best with that which is identifiable and recognizable, rather than that which is amorphous and intangible. We should make all practical efforts to reduce uncertainty, concentrating on those things which lie within our control. In some cases, there may be no obvious action possible. It helps to talk the whole matter through with someone sympathetic, and if no course of action is identifiable, then a positive decision to shelve the whole subject for the time being may be appropriate.

Making decisions is a source of stress for many people. There is no way of anticipating all possibilities, but basic planning, using a pen and paper to help create order, is a good first step. Start by writing down the nature of the problem, and define the choices that seem to exist. One important choice should not be overlooked; that is the positive decision to do nothing. Having defined the problem and all the reasonable alternatives, spend a little time considering unusual alternatives. (This is known as lateral thinking. Most decisions are based on linear thinking, which involves starting at a given point and working towards a desired objective, and this is the best way of dealing with everyday problems). Having an ideal end result in mind also helps, and this should be written down too. Usually, only a limited number of choices exists, and the relative merits and demerits of these should be written down. Finally, a compromise will probably have to be accepted, for seldom is an ideal solution possible if a decision has been creating anxiety. Once it is made, remember that there is always room for modification if the decision does not prove to be as successful as hoped. For example, a widow, living alone and not well enough to take care of herself has two married children living in different areas. Both want her to come to live with, or near, them. Whichever she chooses, the other will feel slighted (or so she believes). What is to be done? She could either stay where she is, or go to one or other of the children. A compromise would be to spend a time with each, or perhaps to choose an alternative companion with whom to share a home. No solution is ideal, but what is vital is to make the most desirable (or the least undesirable) choice and to see what transpires. A further move is always possible if the first choice fails. It is the initial indecision that creates the stress. Once a decision is made, the relative strain and stress is much reduced.

Negative emotions, long held and often unexpressed, can eat away at a person and produce great harm. Much stress is generated because of long held resentments or grudges relating to real or imagined upsets, often years in the past. One way of releasing the tensions locked up in these 'emotional cul-de-sacs', is by means of what can be called 'forgiveness therapy'. If there is anyone of whom the very thought produces a marked degree of tension, then there is probably a suitable case for the use of such therapy. In the first place, one has to realize that whatever happened lies in the past, and that *nothing* can change this. Secondly, it should be realized that holding on to a negative emotional charge over something which is past, harms only yourself, which is hardly sensible. Whatever the circumstances, it is always possible to wipe the slate clean, and to mentally come to terms with what has happened. If practical, this can be accompanied by expressing the forgiveness openly to the individual involved, either verbally or in writing. A common reaction to such a suggestion is: 'But I don't want to reopen contact. That relationship is over and done with.' The truth of the matter is that the relationship is very much alive as long as it continues to hold such a degree of emotional power as to make the very idea of contact repugnant. It will only be over and done with when the emotion resulting from the possibility of such contact is one of indifference; and this will happen only when the other party has been forgiven. Contact is unnecessary, indeed such emotion is often directed towards persons long since dead. There have been cases of Jews, for example, who survived the holocaust and who retained an understandable, but damaging (to themselves) hatred of Germany and all things German. When such individuals can find it in their hearts to forgive the acts committed during the war, a transformation often takes place, which borders on the religious, and which indeed might come more easily to the individual who has faith in a higher power; this is not, however, essential.

Personal relationships also provide a major source of stressful encounters. The more we can come to understand why we behave as we do and why others behave as they do, the easier it becomes to defuse uncomfortable and stress-inducing relationships. This principle forms the basis of a system known as 'transactional analysis'. In his book on the subject, *I'm O.K. – You're O.K.*, Dr Thomas Harris explains that in each of us there exists three states. It is as if in each adult person there co-exists the same little person he was when he was three years old as well as a 'state' relating to his parents. Furthermore, there are 'recordings' in the brain of actual experiences of internal and external events, the most significant of which happened during the first five years of life. Dr Harris goes on to describe a third state (the first two are known as 'child' and 'parent'), which is called 'adult'. These psychological states interact and influence all decisions and relationships and it pays the individual to learn to recognize the 'child' and 'parent' elements in his behaviour. Childlike thought, it is said, manifests itself in doubts, fears and feelings of vulnerability, with behaviour such as crying, tantrums, giggling and shoulder shrugging. 'Parent-like' attitudes manifest themselves in fixed positions, scolding, warning and injunctions, with behaviour such as frowning, pointing of the index finger, looking 'horrified', folding the arms across the chest, sighing, and so on.

The 'adult state' is likened to a computer, which makes decisions after weighing the information derived from the 'child' and the 'parent' and all the data which has been gathered by a lifetime of experience. In dealing with others, it pays to try to recognize these types manifesting themselves. If the 'child' aspect of someone is evident, then by respecting this and talking in a soothing way (just as if dealing with a child) you will reduce the chance of creating stress; for it is not childish to manifest the 'child' aspect, but is simply evidence of a degree of insecurity in the particular circumstances.

If you find that you are quick to take offence, then apply the old adage of 'counting to 10' for this allows time for the 'adult' in you to assess the information and to sort out the validity, or otherwise, of the initial ('parent' or 'child') reaction. In this respect, it is always best to say nothing rather than something of which you are not sure, or which you know to be a 'child' or 'parent' reaction. Of course, everyone should be prepared to listen to criticism of himself without reacting to the *fact* of criticism. Listen to what is being said, evaluate it, and then either modify your behaviour or explain the reasons for it. This attitude will avoid stressful confrontations as well as providing insights into how other people see you. Bear in mind that a major stress factor may be seen as the difference which lies between the real world and the world as the individual would wish it. His fantasy of how things ought to be, is much influenced by 'parent' and 'child' attitudes. If the 'adult' can take control of the situation and apply the understanding gained through experience, then reactions would be less aberrant and stressful.

In modifying your life-style to reduce stress, it is worth examining habits other than just smoking and drinking. For example, one can get into the habit of looking serious, unsmiling and severe when, in fact, it is just as easy to look carefree and to smile. The strange fact is that our emotions will respond to the way we look, just as the opposite situation is true. A friendly word, a smile, active interest in others, tolerance and praise rather than criticism, all lead to a feedback of warmth and happiness, and can enormously reduce stress both at home and at work. What is the image you have of yourself and does it correspond to the image others have of you? If there is a lack of harmony in your environment, then it is possible that you are projecting an unhappy, stress-inducing image. The changes in thinking and behaviour that are required, need effort, but the results are worth it.

One vital point is that we have to learn to accept that which cannot be changed; attempts must be made to minimize the effects of *inevitably* stressful episodes in life by means of relaxation techniques and personal development. Since it has been estimated that 85 per cent of all symptoms represent a reaction to stress, and that much illness is, at least partly, caused by the emotions, it is obviously crucial to be able to control them to a certain extent.

One frequent reaction to suggestions that an individual might do best to change his behaviour is: 'that's the way I am, I can't change'. This is plainly an evasion of that which is most desirable, i.e. a modification to a less stress-inducing mode of behaviour. Change is always possible, and the way to start is to recognize the nature of the problem. A kleptomaniac may realize that, ultimately, his behaviour will lead to arrest and disgrace. The desire to avoid this may cause a determined effort to overcome the urge to steal. The end result will be added stress and the likelihood that the urge will nevertheless overcome the fear of punishment. On the other hand, if insight could be gained as to *why* the individual is a klepto-maniac, not only would the desired change begin to take place, but it would be achieved without stress. The key to painlessly changing behaviour patterns lies in *understanding the reasons for such behaviour*. To achieve these insights may well require psychotherapy in one of its many guises.

8. The Role of Psychotherapy
All disease is connected in some way with the emotional,

psychic or mental make-up of the individual. Treatment by psychotherapy does not follow a uniform pattern. There are a wide variety of methods, all aimed at achieving an insight on the part of the patient as to the cause of his particular health problem. Such obvious symptoms as depression, phobias, neurosis, etc. lend themselves to psychotherapy more obviously than do such conditions as colitis, arthritis, hypertension, diabetes or ulcers. Yet all these conditions can frequently be shown to contain a large psychosomatic component, i.e. the mind affecting the body.

As we shall see in the section on 'guided imagery', or visualization, the main principle works two ways. If negative emotions can have adverse effects on health, so can positive images and thoughts have beneficial effects on health and well-being. Whether the psychotherapeutic method used is a traditional, one-to-one, psycho-analytical approach, or a form of group therapy which is monitored by a trained therapist, or one of the more recent forms of 'humanistic' psychotherapy, the objectives are much the same. These are to reveal aspects of the individual to him or herself and, via these insights, to enable him to cope more adequately with life. In the process, the various symptoms would be expected to improve or vanish or, at the very least, to not get any worse.

The success of these methods depends, to a large extent, on the attitude and co-operation of the patient, who should be prepared for insights which are not always pleasant. A programme of individual sessions with a therapist and/or group sessions may continue for many months, or even years, at intervals varying from three times a week to once a week, depending on the needs of the case. In many cases, a successful resolution can be achieved in a matter of months – much depends upon the attitude of the patient and the degree of rapport with the therapist, as well as the suitability of the particular form of psychotherapy employed.

There is no particular condition which responds to a particular form of psychotherapy. Indeed, the field is so varied that no specific advice can be given as to such a choice. The individual should seek a positive, constructive approach to his problems in all schools of psychotherapy.

Group therapies offer the opportunity for people with

varied backgrounds to compare and discuss their own circumstances and to observe each other's attitudes, feelings and
conditions. In a much simpler manner, the group activities of
Alcoholics Anonymous and Weight Watchers are based on the
same idea of mutual support and release from isolation. In
psychoanalysis, a far more detailed examination is made on a
one-to-one basis, of the origins of the individual's problems.
Insights obtained by both these methods often lead to the
resolution of deep-seated emotional problems.

'Encounter' is a system which grew out of the work of an
American psychologist, Kurt Lewin, who devised ways of
enhancing personal awareness and personality development
through training, emphasizing contact between people. This
system was developed during the fifties and sixties and is now
employed in a number of ways. An 'encounter' group with a
trained leader provides the opportunity for breaking down
inhibitions and learning to take personal responsibility, thus
achieving greater understanding of oneself, and therefore of
others.

A system known as sensitivity training was developed in
America in the late 1940's. This is also known as Training
Group Therapy, made up of groups of seven to fifteen people
who work together to assist in gaining insights into personality
and behaviour.

A variation of this is called 'psychodrama', in which
participants spontaneously act out dramatic roles, in the
presence of a skilled therapist, in order to gain insights into
deeply hidden feelings and attitudes. The roles might be those
of conflict or stress, real or imagined, from the individual's
past, present or future. This was a development of a Viennese
contemporary of Freud's, the psychiatrist, Jacob Moreno.

A method developed by the American psychotherapist,
Arthur Janov Ph.D., is classified as 'primal' therapy. This
means that it attempts to recall or realize stresses and tensions
repressed since early childhood. To this end, Janov assists his
patients in regressing to their infancy. Other 'primal' methods
also aim at regression to childhood or to birth experience, and
can even induce traumas associated with experiences in the
womb. These systems might employ dream analysis or
hypnosis. New 'primal' therapies see the release of long held

stresses as a natural process, which can take place once patients are encouraged to stop holding back or repressing the free expression of their basic needs.

Another recent school of psychotherapeutic thought is that known as *Gestalt* therapy. This evolved from the work of Dr Frederick Perls, who developed his theories in the late 1950's in America. Analysis of the individual and interpretation of his symptoms and problems are avoided. The methods employed here aim at helping the individual to recognize that many aspects of his behaviour pattern, which once served a supportive purpose, are no longer relevant and, indeed, may have become an obstacle to well-being. Attention is paid to the way the individual expresses his needs and attitudes. Body postures and movements, voice tone, physical tensions, etc., are seen as presenting vital clues to underlying stresses. By learning the meaning of these, and learning to release them, a degree of personal growth occurs. The *Gestalt* therapist may employ a variety of other disciplines, notably 'bio-energetics' and 'transactional analysis'. A key aspect of *Gestalt* therapy is to bring the individual into the present, and to enable the moment to be enjoyed to the full. Suppressed emotions and inhibitions once again have to be released in order to achieve this. 'Bio-energetics' is a system which developed out of the original work of Wilhelm Reich M.D. in America. It aims to bring about the healthy integration of mind and body by releasing physical tensions which accompany all psychological or emotional problems. The methods used are complex and sometimes extremely vigorous, incorporating breathing techniques, postural restructuring and the release of long held muscular stress patterns, which vary in each individual. Psychosynthesis is a system which developed from the work of the Italian psychiatrist, Roberto Assagioli, and which aims at integrating various aspects of the personality.

Many of these methods have been incorporated into the Humanistic Psychology Association, the aim of which is to realize a level of health above the normal conception in which health is seen simply as the absence of disease. Hopefully, by drawing on the valid systems mentioned above, and others of a similar nature, a synthesis of what is most useful can be found. Some methods are more suitable as a way of achieving 'growth' or 'awareness', and others are more obviously suited to releasing the stresses of the disturbed individual. All these methods have in common the over-riding interest in the patient and not the symptoms. Whether the manifestation of the psychiatric stress takes the form of physical symptoms such as high blood pressure, or psychological symptoms such as phobias, neurosis, etc., it is the underlying causes which are dealt with rather than the symptoms.

In making use of the chapters which follow, the objective should be, within a few months, to be able to give a positive answer to all, or at least most of the following questions:

1. Do you feel well?
2. Do you sleep well and wake refreshed?
3. Do you like most people?
4. Do you look forward to the future with confidence?
5. Do you enjoy life?
6. Are you normally relaxed and happy?
7. Are you regularly eating a balanced diet?
8. Do you exercise regularly?
9. Are you happy about your appearance?
10. Are you enjoying a mutually satisfactory emotional and/or sexual relationship?

The potentials for individuals to develop and grow as personalities are almost limitless. We have untapped resources and reserves, which most of us are never even aware of. Health and happiness are the most precious commodities on earth. The following chapters present an opportunity to acquire them.

5.

Relaxation Exercises

Before attempting meditation or visualization techniques (see the following chapters), it is suggested that at least one of the relaxation measures outlined in this chapter should be mastered and practised. This will greatly enhance the effect of more advanced techniques.

There are two primary areas of bodily function which are, to a degree, under conscious control, and which we can use to modify arousal, i.e. reduce stress. Recall the effects on the body of stress, in the 'fight or flight' situation (see page 24). One of the first things to happen is a tensing of the voluntary muscles, in preparation for anticipated action. At the same moment, there is an increase in the rate of breathing to meet the extra demand for oxygen made by these muscles. In attempting to relax and calm a chronic state of arousal, it is towards these two functions that attention should be directed. It is possible to interfere with the stress cycle at other points, for example, by using biofeedback methods (see page 98); through this it is possible to learn to lower the blood pressure, slow the heart rate, alter the skin temperature, etc. Valuable as such methods are, they are simply examples of learning to control functions of the body which are normally beyond conscious control.

Critics of relaxation exercises claim that they do not fully instruct the individual in awareness and correct use of his body. Systems such as the 'Alexander technique' take many months, and often years, to teach correct use of the body and how to most efficiently and effortlessly perform any task or movement. This excellent system might well be undertaken by the individual aiming for a tension-free existence as a step towards that ideal. However, it is very time-consuming, drawn out and expensive. Whilst acknowledging that relaxation and other means of stress-proofing outlined in this book will not achieve a re-education of the individual's use of his body, these relatively simple, safe and cheap methods, requiring only a little regular practice, *will* produce improvement in function, reduction of stress and greater well-being. If the individual still wishes to continue to improve on this, then an Alexander teacher should be contacted. It is also suggested that structural evaluation and, if necessary, treatment, be undertaken by a qualified osteopath to ensure that any areas of mechanical restriction, especially in the spinal and pelvic regions, are corrected prior to starting relaxation techniques.

In the initial stages, it is best to practise one or other of the relaxation methods at least once, and ideally twice daily for five to fifteen minutes. Once you have tried all the methods several times each, you should be aware of which suits you best. The chosen method or methods should then be employed and practised twice daily in a quiet environment. When proficient, it will be found that this regular practice will enable you to apply the technique in any situation. Application of one of the relaxation methods when in a potentially tense or stressful situation will markedly unwind you, and reduce the physical and psychological effects which would normally become evident. Such things as stage fright, interview and exam 'nerves', frustration in a traffic jam or when late for an appointment, anger during an argument, etc., can all be reduced to a mild, controlled reaction by the introduction of such techniques.

The environment in which relaxation exercises are practised should be quiet and not unduly warm or cold. The surface on which the exercise is performed should be firm but not so hard as to be uncomfortable, or so soft as to induce sleep. A blanket on a carpeted floor is perhaps the ideal surface. Clothing should be loose, with no constricting or distracting elements. Remove shoes, ties, etc.; undo bras and belts. Lying on the back is the ideal position, with a small neck pillow and a bolster or cushion under the knees if the back is more comfortable that way. (Anyone who has a history of low-back strain, or who has a hollow back, will probably be more comfortable with the knees slightly flexed in this way). Sitting in a supported position is suggested if there is any tendency to fall asleep when in the lying position. Some adepts at yoga prefer the cross-legged or lotus position, and others prefer to kneel, using a small stool to support the buttocks. Whichever position is chosen, the only essential aspect as far as the first two exercises are concerned, is that you are comfortable. Later exercises will specify if a particular position is desirable. Falling asleep during the performance of any exercise is to be avoided since the aim is to practise and experience something *consciously*.

There should be no distracting sounds such as radio or T.V. during the relaxation period, and no sense of urgency should be felt. It is probably best *not* to attempt such exercises too soon after eating a meal. Morning and evening seem to be times that suit most people. Once you have introduced your routine, endeavour not to miss practising the exercises, for it is only by persistent repetition that the first stages of relaxation will be mastered, leading on to deep relaxation and other methods of 'mind control'. At first, it may appear that nothing much is happening. Indeed, the tense individual probably believes deep down that such simple measures, helpful as they may be to others, are not for him with his superactive mind which just cannot relax. Patient, persistent and thorough application will satisfy even this Type A individual that the methods are worthwhile.

When you begin to practise any of the exercises, you will find that intrusive thoughts come periodically into the mind to interrupt the smooth flow of the techniques. This is normal and to be expected. It should not produce any reaction of distress or anger. When a thought intrudes, push it *gently* to one side and resume the exercise. It does not matter how frequently such interruptions occur, simply carry on where you left off. Gradually, week by week, there will be fewer interruptions and relaxation will deepen. Whichever exercise is being used, there should be an awareness that there is no 'correct' response. Your body and your mind will respond *your* way. Be passive, do not try to 'force' the exercise. Relaxation comes at its own speed. Be an observer of the processes taking place; sense changes which occur in a detached way. Let things happen and register your thoughts and feelings. Above all, be patient and passive.

1. *Rhythmic Abdominal Breathing*
Whilst learning the technique, arrange to have two free
periods per day, each of five to fifteen minutes. Find a quiet
room where you know you will not be disturbed. Rest on your
back, head and shoulders slightly raised, pillow under the
knees to take the strain off them and off your back. Rest your
hands on the upper abdomen, close your eyes, settle down in a
comfortable position. See that there is nothing in the way where
you are lying or in the room that is going to distract your attention, such as sunlight, a clock, animals, and so on. Sitting in a
reclining position is also suitable, and many people prefer this
to lying down. Try both, and choose whichever is most
comfortable.

Breathing is of great value in relaxation, particularly during
the initial stages. The person who is at ease with himself and
the world breathes slowly, deeply and rhythmically. Breathing
is the only automatic function which one is capable of
controlling. It is carried out partly through the autonomic
nervous system and partly through the central nervous
system. The autonomic nervous system is that which controls
vital functions, endocrine (hormone) secretions and emotions.
By controlling one's breathing, one can influence all these
and, for a short time, take over conscious responsibility for
them.

The aim is to breathe slowly, deeply and rhythmically. You
cannot expect to do this perfectly to begin with – it might even
take weeks. Inhale through the nose slowly and deeply. The
abdomen, on which the hands are resting, should rise gently
as the breathing begins. An awareness of this rising and falling
of the abdomen is important to establish that the diaphragm is
being used properly. The inhalation should be slow, unforced
and unhurried. Whilst breathing in, silently and slowly, count
to four, five or six. When the inhalation is complete, pause for
two or three seconds, then slowly exhale through the nose. As
you exhale, you should feel the abdomen slowly descend.
Count this breathing out, as you did when breathing in.
(Again, a count of four, five or six should be achieved). *The
exhalation should take at least as long as the inhalation.*

There should be no sense of strain regarding the breathing
cycle. If, at first, you feel you have breathed to your fullest

capacity by a count of three, then so be it. Try to gradually slow down the rhythm until a slow count of five or six is possible, both on inhalation and exhalation, with a pause of two or three seconds between each change.

Remember to start each breath with an upward push of the abdomen. With the mind thus occupied on the mechanics of the breathing, as described above, as well as on the rhythmic counting, there is little scope for thinking about anything else. Nevertheless, initially at least, extraneous thoughts will intrude. This pattern of breathing should be repeated fifteen to twenty times and, since each cycle should take about fifteen seconds, this exercise should occupy a total of about five minutes.

It is suggested that during the exercise, once the mechanics and counting have become well established as a pattern, it is useful to introduce a variety of thoughts during different phases of the cycle. For example, on inhalation try to sense a feeling of warmth and energy entering the body with the air. On exhaling, sense a feeling of sinking and settling deeper into the supporting surface. An overall sense of warmth and heaviness accompanying the repetitive breathing cycle will effectively begin the relaxation process. Physiologically, this exercise will slow down the heart rate, reduce sympathetic nervous activity, relax tense muscles and allow a chance for the balancing, restoratative, parasympathetic nervous function, to operate, as well as calming the mind. In the initial stages, this might be sufficient exercise for one session. When proficient, it can be used to precede one of the other relaxation methods and, later, in a shortened version of, say eight to ten breathing cycles, one of the meditation or visualization techniques.

After completion of the exercise, do not get up immediately but rest for a minute or two, allowing the mind to become aware of any sensations of stillness, warmth, heaviness, etc. Once mastered, this exercise can be used in any tense situation with the certainty that it will defuse the normal agitated response and should result in a far greater ability to cope.

2. *Breathing and Repeated Sound Technique*
Sit or lie in a comfortable position in a suitable room. Close your eyes and encourage a sense of heaviness and stillness. Focus your attention on the body, area by area, briefly, in

order to assess them for obvious tension. Start with the feet and pass on to the lower legs, thighs, hips, buttocks, abdomen, lower back, chest, shoulders, neck, face, arms and hands. Do not overlook the eyes and jaw muscles. Many people screw up the eye muscles or clench the jaw habitually. If this is one of your traits, then pay particular attention to releasing these areas prior to continuing with the exercise.

This should only be a brief survey, not lasting for more than a few seconds in each region. As each area is visualized, any obvious tension should be released. If you are not sure whether a muscle or area is relaxed, tense it for a few seconds and then let it go. This brief but effective progressive muscular relaxation, area by area, prepares you for the exercise properly. It is worth emphasizing that relaxation is a passive act. You cannot 'try' to relax, for this is a contradiction in terms. Relaxation is a letting go, a switching off, which ideally involves no effort. In suggesting that dubious areas be tensed prior to 'letting go', this is only to help to imprint on the mind the contrast between the two states. In this way, a gradual awareness will develop, enabling you to sense tension as it arises and, most importantly, to release it. (This is the basis of progressive muscular relaxation methods, and they will be described more fully in exercise no. 4). For the purposes of this exercise, the abbreviated method outlined above is all that is required as preparation for the following breathing method.

Having spent a minute or, at most, two in 'letting go' the obvious areas of tension in the musculature of the body, begin to breathe in and out through the nose. Passively pay attention to your breathing and, as you breathe out, say *silently* and slowly to yourself any one-syllable word. Breathe in and out at any comfortable speed; there need be no rush, nor is there any need to make the breathing particularly slow. The rhythm should be as natural and unforced as possible, not particularly deep or unusually shallow. You may well find that the rhythm will alter from time to time, or that, periodically, you will let out a very deep breath or sigh. Just let it happen, do not attempt to control the rhythm or depth of the respiration – simply use it to time the repetitive, slow enunciation of a word or sound. Many people use the word 'one' for this purpose, but any short word will do. Remember it should be said as you breathe out. This should continue for about ten minutes.

A feeling of stillness and calm should eventually be felt. In some cases, a sense of happiness and deep relaxation is quickly achieved. In others, there is only a gradual sense of being less stressed. In all cases, where this type of exercise is performed as described, positive physiological changes will take place, irrespective of subjective feelings. In other words, *there is a degree of stress reduction, whether or not you sense it, from the outset.* Many people expect immediate, obvious change. If disappointed in this expectation, they may abandon the discipline involved in the regular performance of these exercises. This is sad and a waste, for it has been positively established that the benefits of the exercises often begin long before there is any awareness of improvement..

The repetition of the chosen word may well be interrupted periodically by intrusive thoughts. When this happens, do not feel irritated, simply resume the use of the word to coincide with exhalation. Each individual will reap the benefits of this exercise at his own pace.

After about ten minutes of this exercise, stop repeating the word and simply allow the mind the luxury of doing nothing. Allow it to linger in the still, peaceful state to which you have drifted. Initially with the eyes closed and later with them open, spend at least two minutes in this state of inactivity. Slowly get up and resume your normal activities. (It is unwise to get up too quickly after exercise 1 or 2, as over-oxygenation may result in transient giddiness.)

3. *Short Alternate Nostril Breathing*
There are a number of variations in applying this simple technique which has its origins in yoga. At its simplest, the right thumb is placed against the right nostril, the right index and middle fingers against the forehead, and the right ring finger against the left nostril. (Reverse all instructions if you wish to use the left hand, i.e. left thumb on left nostril, etc). By pressing lightly with the thumb, close the passage of air on the right side of the nose and inhale slowly and deeply up the left nostril. Pause for a moment between inhalation and exhalation. During this pause, press lightly on the left side of the nose whilst releasing the thumb pressure on the right. Breathe out

down the right side. Maintain the hand position and breathe in again through the right side. Again, between inhaling and exhaling, pause momentarily and reverse the pressure, so that the next exhalation is again through the left nostril. Continue as above.

Refinements of this basic technique include counting slowly to three on inhalation, pausing for a count of two, and then exhaling to a count of six. By focusing on the simple mechanics and the counting rhythm, a degree of distraction from current problems takes place. This cycle of alternate breathing can be repeated between five and twenty times. In most cases, a sense of ease and 'letting go' takes place after about seven cycles. This exercise does not replace either of the first two exercises, but is a first-aid measure to be used any time, in any position, in addition to other methods, whenever a feeling of stress or anxiety is felt.

4. *Progressive Muscular Relaxation*
This method involves the systematic, conscious relaxation of all the body areas, in sequence. The position for this exercise should be reclining – either on the floor or on a recliner-type chair. Ideally, there should be no distracting sounds and the clothing worn should not constrict in any way. (A few cycles of deep breathing should precede the exercise).

Starting with the feet, try to sense or feel that the muscles of the area are not actively tense. Then deliberately tighten them, curling the toes under and holding the tension for five to ten seconds. Then tense the muscles *even more strongly*, for a further few seconds before letting all the tension go and sensing the wonderful feeling of release. Try to consciously register what this feels like, especially in comparison with the tense state in which you have been holding them. Progress to the calf muscles and exercise them in the same way. First sense the state the muscles are in, then tense them, hold the position, and then tense them even more before letting go. Positively register the sense of release. In doing this to the leg muscles, there is a slight danger of inducing cramp. If this occurs, then stop tensing that area immediately and move on to the next. After the calf muscles, go on to exercise the knees, then the upper leg, thigh muscles, the buttocks, the lower and upper back, the abdomen, the chest, the shoulders, the arms and hands, and then the neck, head and face. The precise sequence is irrelevant, as long as all these areas are 'treated' to the tensing, the extra tensing, and then the release.

Some areas need extra attention in this respect. The abdominal region is a good example. The tensing of these muscles can be achieved in either contraction (i.e. a pulling in of the muscles), or by stretching (i.e. pushing outwards of the muscles). This variation in tensing method is applicable to many of the body's muscles. Indeed, at different times, it is a good idea to vary the pattern, and instead of, for example, contracting and tensing a muscle group, try to stretch and tense them to their limit. This is especially useful in the muscles of the face, particularly in the mouth and eye region. Individual attention to these is important. On one occasion it would be desirable, for example, for the 'tensing' of the mouth muscles to take the form of holding the mouth open as widely as possible, with the lips tense during this phase. On a subsequent occasion, the 'tensing' could be a tight-pursed pressing together of the lips. If there is time available, both methods of tensing can be employed during the same exercise, especially in the areas you know to be very tense. The muscles controlling the jaw, eyes, mouth, tongue and neck are particularly important, as are the abdominal muscles, since much emotional tension is reflected in these regions, and release and relaxation often has profound·effects.

There are between twenty and twenty-five of these 'areas', depending upon how you go about interpreting the guidelines given above; each should involve at least five to ten seconds of tensing and a further five to ten seconds of 'letting go' and of passively sensing that feeling. Thus, eight to ten minutes should suffice for the successful completion of this whole technique. This should be followed by several minutes of an unhurried return to a feeling of warm, relaxed tranquility. Focus the mind on the whole body. Try to sense it as heavy and content, free of tension or effort. This might be enhanced by a few cycles of deep breathing. Stretch out like a cat, and then resume your normal activities.

5. *Autogenic-type Exercises*

True autogenic exercises need to be taught by a special teacher or practitioner, well versed in this excellent system. The modified method outlined below is loosely based on the work of the pioneer in this field, Dr H. Schultz. The distinction between a relaxation exercise and a meditation technique is blurred at all times, but never more so than in autogenic methods which are a blend of the two. At least fifteen and ideally twenty minutes should be given to the performance of this method. At another time of the day, this or another relaxation method should also be performed. This routine should become a welcome, eagerly anticipated oasis of calm and peace in the daily programme. Stress-proofing, without such periods of 'switching off', is not likely to be successfully achieved.

A reclining position should be adopted, with the eyes closed. External, distracting sounds should be minimized. The exercises involve the use of specific, verbalized messages to focus awareness on a particular area. *No effort is involved*, but simply a passive concentration on any sensations or emotions which may result from each message. Imagination or auto-suggestion has been found to have definite physiological effects. By combining a sequence of autogenic (i.e. self-generated) instructions with the passive, focused aspect of meditation techniques, a powerful method of self-help has been created.

The exercise starts with a general thought, such as 'I am relaxed and at peace with myself'. Begin to breathe deeply in and out. Feel the light movement of the diaphragm and feel calm.

Stage I: The mind should focus on the area of the body to which the thought is directed. Start by silently verbalizing 'my right arm is heavy'. Think of the image of the right arm. Visualize it completely relaxed, and resting on its support (floor, arm of the chair, etc.). Dissociate it from the body, and from will-power. See the limp, detached arm as being heavy, having *weight*. After a few seconds the phrase should be repeated. This should be done a number of times, before proceeding to the right leg, left leg, left arm, neck, shoulders and back. At each area, try to sense heaviness and maintain a passive feeling in the process.

Stage II: Again, begin with the right arm, concentrating on it as you silently verbalize 'My right arm is warm'. Repeat this and pause to sense warmth in the arm or hand. Repeat this several times. The pause should be unhurried. To encourage this feeling of warmth, it may be useful to imagine that the sun's rays are shining onto the back of the hand, warming it. The sensation of warmth spreads from there to the whole arm.

Proceed through all areas of the body, pausing for some seconds at each to assess sensations which may become apparent. Such changes as occur cannot be controlled, but will happen when the mind is in a passive, receptive state. This exercise increases the peripheral flow of blood, and relaxes the muscles controlling the blood vessels. It is possible to measurably increase the temperature of an area of the body, using these simple methods.

Stage III: This focuses on the breathing cycle with the phrase 'My breathing is calm and regular'. No conscious effort should be made to control the breathing. Unlike the form of breathing used in the exercise on page 85, this involves a passive approach. You should direct your concentration to the slight, even motion of the diaphragm. Nothing should be consciously done about the breathing, which should be completely automatic. Sometimes the verbalized statement can be altered to 'The breathing is calm', or 'I am being breathed', to good effect. Sometimes, quite unconsciously, a deep breath is taken during the otherwise shallow breathing. This is quite normal. Nothing should be done to control the pattern. Simply repeat the chosen phrase, and passively observe and experience the sensations that accompany it. Slow repetition of the phrase promotes deep, slow, regular breathing without effort. Continue for several minutes, repeating the phrase periodically.

Stage IV: The phrase 'My forehead is cool' is repeated for several minutes. This appears to produce a combination of alertness and relaxation. When repeating this phrase, with suitable pauses, try to sense the coolness as a pleasant sensation.

Stage V: The phrase 'I am alert and refreshed' ends the exercise. Breathe deeply, stretch, and continue the day's activities.

During stages I and II, the time spent in each area should not be less than about half a minute; it is, however, quite permissible to spend two or three minutes focusing on any one part, especially if the desired sensation of heaviness or warmth is achieved.

It will probably be found that the desired sensation is more easily sensed in one stage than another, and that some areas seem more 'responsive' than others. This is normal. *It is also quite normal for there to be no subjective appreciation of any of the verbalized sensations.* Do not worry about this. Even if nothing at all is sensed for some considerable time, even some months, there is a great deal actually taking place within the body as a result of the whole exercise. Persistence, patience and a total lack of urgency is all that is necessary for this method to lead to a decrease in muscular tension and a sense of calm and well-being. A 'side-effect' of this particular method is frequently experienced in terms of much improved peripheral circulation, i.e. an end to cold hands and feet!

6.
Additional Relaxation Methods

Hydrotherapy

The use of water in the treatment of a variety of conditions has evolved over the past century. Although taken for granted, water is a highly complex and vital compound. Water has a high specific heat. This means that it gives out or takes in more heat for each degree of change in its own temperature than any other substance. Water also has the ability to conduct heat more efficiently than most other liquids. A variety of forms of hydrotherapy exist, and these can be summarized as those that have a physical effect, due to pressure or mechanical stimulation (hydrokinetic), those that alter temperature (hydrothermal), and those that have a chemical effect due to the constituents of the water (hydrochemical).

Neutral Bath

There are many nerve endings on the skin surface and these deal with the reception of stimuli. More of these are cold receptors than heat receptors. If water of a different temperature to that of the skin is applied, it will either conduct heat to it or absorb heat from it. Such stimuli have an influence on the sympathetic nervous system and can affect the hormonal system. The greater the difference between the temperature of the skin and the water applied, the greater will be the potential for physiological reaction. Conversely, water that is the same temperature as the body has a marked relaxing and sedative effect on the nervous system. This is of value in states of stress, and has led to the development of the so-called 'neutral bath'.

Before the development and use of tranquillizing drugs, the most dependable and effective method of calming an agitated patient was the use of a neutral bath. The patient was placed in a tub of water, the temperature of which was maintained at between 33.5°C and 35.6°C (92 to 96°F), often for over three hours and sometimes for up to twenty-four hours. This is obviously not a practical proposition for the average tense individual. As a self-help measure, the neutral bath does, however, offer a means of sedating the nervous system if used for relatively short periods. It is important to maintain the water temperature at the level indicated, and a bath thermo- meter should be obtained from a chemist. The air temperature of the bathroom should be sufficiently high to avoid any sense of chilliness. Half an hour immersed in such a bath will have a sedative or even a soporific effect. It places no strain on the heart, circulation or nervous system, and achieves muscular relaxation and a general vasodilation (relaxation and expansion of the blood vessels); all of these conditions are prerequisites of relaxation. If accompanied by breathing, meditation or visual imagery exercises (see following chapters), a fine combination of approaches towards dealing with the effects of stress will be established. This method may be used daily if necessary.

Hot Bath

A hot bath is one that utilizes water between the temperatures at 36.5°C and 40°C (98°F to 104°F). It is useful as a means of muscle relaxation, which is vital to the overall relaxation process. Five minutes immersion at this temperature is adequate to begin with. If no sensation of weakness or other untoward symptoms result, then increase the daily duration until ten minutes daily is reached. It is important to realize that a brief hot bath has quite a different effect from a long one. Nothing is to be gained by prolonging such a bath in the hope of achieving greater benefit. Immersion in hot water acts not only on the surface nerves but also on the autonomic nervous system (that part that is normally outside the control of the individual), and on the hormone-producing glands, particu- larly the adrenals, which become less active. Generally speaking, a hot bath is sedative, although a *long* hot bath will have the opposite effect. (Some individuals will find the hot bath more effective than the neutral bath in achieving some degree of relaxation).

Jacuzzi or Whirlpool Bath

This is a bath in which the temperature of the water can be controlled, in addition to there being a degree of agitation of the water by means of an electric agitator or jets of compressed air. The effect is of combined heat and massage. If the temperature is maintained at a little below 36°C, a relaxing effect will be achieved by ten to twenty minutes immersion.

Herbal Infusions

In all of the above-mentioned baths, additional benefit may be obtained by the use of medical or aromatic herbs in the water. Chamomile, valerian, rosemary and lime blossom, are all useful. The herb (usually 1 oz/25g of the dried herb to 1 pint ½ litre of water) is boiled, and then allowed to stand for fifteen minutes. The liquid strained from this should be added to the bath. The therapeutic effects of these herbs are achieved by means of inhalation and absorption through the skin, which has been shown to be less impermeable than was previously thought.

Sauna

This Finnish method of sitting or lying in a dry, hot room for varying lengths of time *appears* to have a relaxing effect. In effect though, the actual physiological benefits of this are minimal in terms of stress reduction. In fact, the physiological stress involved in coping with temperatures of between 75 and 100°C is so profound that this system is only suitable for the very healthy. There is some slight overall reduction in the metabolic rate after a sauna. A significant decrease in blood pressure takes place in the majority of cases after a sauna, but in 12.5 per cent of cases there is an overall *increase* in blood pressure. All in all, it would seem that saunas should be used only by individuals with a clean bill of health who are not highly stressed, and even then only in moderation. The 'relaxed' state, claimed by adherents, is probably a mild state of exhaustion.

Turkish Baths

These differ from saunas in that the degree of humidity used is far higher. The same general observations apply, though, despite this difference. These systems are fairly well tolerated by healthy individuals, but are not advisable for anyone with health problems, and it must be remembered that anyone in a stressed state has a health problem. When stressed, the response of the body can be unpredictable, and the addition of periods of intense heat can only be seen as a further stress factor.

Cold Packs

Cold packs were described by the famous nineteenth century Bavarian pastor, Sebastian Kneipp in his famous treatise *My Water Cure*, in which he explained the advantages of hydrotherapy. A cold pack is actually a warm pack, but derives its name from the cold nature of the initial application.

The requirements are as follows: One piece of cotton material; one piece of flannel or woollen (blanket) material; one plastic or rubber sheet to protect any bedding. The cotton material is soaked in very cold water, then wrung out well and placed on the flannel material, which is spread out on the plastic sheet. The subject lies on the damp material, which is then folded around the trunk and immediately covered by the flannel material; this is then safety-pinned firmly in place. The top bed covers should then be drawn up over the subject, and a hot water bottle is given to him. The initial cold application produces a reaction which draws fresh blood to the surface, and this warmth, being well insulated, is retained by the damp material; a 'warm pack' is produced which, gradually, over a six to eight hour period, bakes itself dry. There may be copious sweating in the process, and the material should be well washed prior to its re-use. The pack can be slept in and should, in fact, help towards a deeper, more refreshing sleep. The overall effect is a calming one. Larger, whole body packs are also used, but they do require assistance in application, and in extricating the subject from the mummy-like wrapping which extends from the armpits to the feet. Should a sensation of damp cold be experienced when a pack is in place, it is usually a result of the material being too wet, or the insulation being inadequate or too loose.

The holistic approach to health insists that the whole man is treated, rather than just his symptoms, and that the treatment itself should not create additional problems for the patient. Hydrotherapy, when used as part of an overall attempt to remove the causes and the effects of stress, fits into the holistic approach.

Biofeedback

Biofeedback is a system which utilizes the 'feedback' to the individual, of biological information, not usually available to him, thus enabling him to learn to exercise control over organs and functions which are normally outside his voluntary control. By means of these techniques, individuals have achieved control over circulatory functions, as evidenced by the ability to increase or decrease the temperature of a particular body area. Other examples include control of the heart rate, blood pressure, gastric secretions, brainwave patterns, skin resistance to electricity, relaxation of muscle groups, and so on. The effects of this system are profound, since such control has previously only been achieved using drug therapy.

In terms of stress and its effects, biofeedback offers a method which enables the individual to learn to control some of its harmful consequences. It is not certain that by learning, for example, to lower blood pressure or to raise skin resistance to electricity (both evidence of a reduction in tension), that *overall* relaxation is achieved. It may be that since only one physiological function is being monitored and controlled at any one time, other stress-induced symptoms might remain unaltered. A further drawback in comparison to meditation and relaxation exercises, is that relatively expensive equipment is required for most biofeedback monitoring. Most individuals, however, can achieve more rapid results by using such equipment than by using relatively slow-acting meditation and relaxation methods.

The simplest biofeedback equipment is that which measures the electrical skin resistance (E.S.R.). Electrode pads are attached to the palm or fingers of either hand. The information derived via the electrodes is fed into a machine; this, in turn, produces a sound which is louder when the E.S.R. is low (indicating anxiety or tension), and softer when it is high (indicating calm and relaxation). The objective is to use the mind to silence the machine. This is achieved by trial and error, until the individual learns what to do to reduce the sound level completely. At this point, a relative state of relaxation will have been achieved.

A similar machine involves the measurement of the skin temperature of a hand or foot. The information may be displayed on a screen or given as a sound signal. As the individual learns what to do to increase the temperature, he will effectively be relaxing the muscles of the limb (since this is what causes the flow of blood to increase and the temperature to rise). This particular method has been used successfully in helping sufferers to 'switch off' headaches at their outset. General relaxation of the area is certainly achieved, but it is not certain that full body relaxation is thus achieved. The control of blood pressure and heart rate can be achieved in a similar way, through mental effort.

What is not certain is whether, in the long-term, the individual, having 'learned' to achieve the desired result whilst attached to biofeedback equipment, can continue to do so in everyday life. Other systems, such as meditation and relaxation techniques, do have the ability to influence everyday experience, as well as allowing the possibility of increased 'awareness' and personality development. Biofeedback cannot, as yet, make similar claims. The best results with biofeedback have been achieved when such methods are combined with meditation and relaxation exercises. Certainly, no biofeedback methods which monitor specific organs or functions should be utilized without supervision if an attempt is being made to modify an existing health problem. Simple biofeedback equipment to monitor E.S.R. or skin temperature is available for around £50. No explicit instructions as to what to do to achieve the desired result, whether it be raising or lowering the temperature, or raising the E.S.R., are provided. The essence of the technique is for the individual to learn, by repetition, what it is that has to be done, using the mind to silence the buzzer or to switch off the light on the machine. It is a system which requires internal experimentation and, initially, the results might well be chaotic, as noises get louder in response to 'wrong' signals. We all learn to function, from infancy onwards, in a very similar manner.

The more advanced biofeedback methods monitor the brainwave patterns. A very expensive piece of technology, known as the 'mind mirror', displays twelve rows of information, analyzing the subject's brain rhythms from both sides of the brain simultaneously. Different patterns of meditation and levels of relaxation can be monitored in this way, and this is certain to be of great value as an aid to stress reduction, if its prohibitive cost can be trimmed sufficiently to make it generally available.

Many hospitals and clinics now utilize biofeedback methods, and anyone with stress problems might suggest to his doctor, that this would be a useful method for controlling his symptoms.

Biofeedback leads to self-awareness. Whether it provides as full an awareness as other systems is debatable, but it is effective, and signifies a breakthrough in understanding the ability to take responsibility for one's own health.

Note: Machines and instructions for their use are available from Audio Ltd, 26 Wendal Rd, London W12 or Aleph One, P.O. Box 72 S, Cambridge.

Eeman's Relaxation Circuits

An amazing piece of research into the curative properties of human radiations was carried out by the late L. E. Eeman. His work was ahead of its time and those interested may investigate further by reading his books *Co-operative Healing* (Frederick Muller Ltd, London, 1947) and *The Technique of Conscious Evolution* (C. W. Daniel, 1956).

In so far as it involves the individuals attempting to reduce stress and induce relaxation, it is worth examining briefly. The method is completely safe and, in my own experience, frequently effective. Firstly, Eeman states that the human body has specific electrical polarities. By repeatedly using the methods described below, as well as many far more complex ones, and by meticulously recording the results, Eeman came to the conclusion that . . .

forces, latent in man, . . . make the nervous system behave as though there were electromagnetic opposition between its top and its bottom, its right and its left sides and its front and back, and as though, on all three planes or axes, there were a gradiant of potential between extreme polar opposites.

Eeman found that by linking different aspects of these polarities in various ways he could establish a 'relaxation circuit'. He is careful to state that although, for convenience, he has named certain areas as positive and others as negative, the reverse is equally likely to be correct. Indeed, he makes it

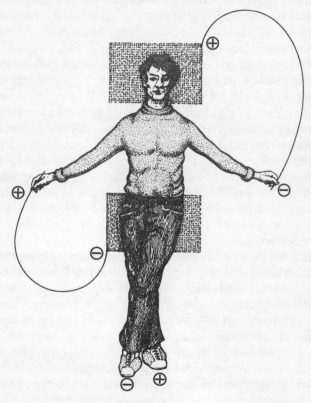

Figure 1

This illustrates one subject in Eeman's relaxation circuit showing copper gauze mats and wire connections. Eeman ignored minor polarity variations and considered (a) the head and base of the spine, (b) the right and left hands, (c) the right and left feet, all as polar opposites. By crossing the feet these poles are 'short-circuited', and the relaxation circuit is created by linking the free positive and negative poles as illustrated.

clear that whilst the observed phenomenon suggests an electrical analogy, and therefore terminology, in fact the phenomenon appears to have more to do with short-wave radiation or magnetic fields, since direct contact with the skin of the area was unnecessary and did not affect the results. His working hypothesis was 'that conducted wireless radiations emitted by the human body can be used therapeutically, provided that polar opposites are linked by electrical conductors'. His classical diagram of human polarities shows the following characteristics:

Positive: Right foot, right hand, left side of head, top of sternum (breastbone) and base of neck area.

Negative: Left foot, left hand, right side of head and base of spine.

Eeman placed the individual on two copper gauze mats, one under the head and one under the sacrum, and then linked the left side of the upper one, by means of a length of copper wire, to the left hand (positive to negative) and the lower one, by similar means, to the right hand (positive to negative). The ankles were kept in a crossed position. Eeman emphasizes that the method should only be used on a relaxed subject. (It is strongly recommended that anyone wishing to promote the deep relaxation and sense of well-being that this method usually brings, first learn to relax by using one or other of the methods described in Chapter 6). Eeman states categorically that 'in the absence of voluntary muscular relaxation, reactions may not only be obscured but frequently reversed'. If a relaxation state is already being achieved via the methods outlined in Chapter 6 or 8, then the use of the 'relaxation circuit' will be found to be most advantageous. Ten minutes is suggested as the minimum, and thirty minutes is the ideal amount of time to spend on this method.

Eeman went on to link, in circuit, ever-increasing numbers of people at the same time. The therapeutic and relaxation effects thus produced are worthy of further research by healing professions. In using the simple circuit described above, nothing but good can result if the individual is (a) relaxed at the outset, and (b) practices the method for ten to thirty minutes per session, at frequent intervals (several times weekly).

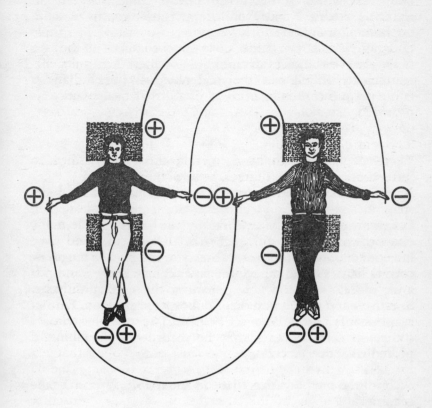

Figure 2

This shows two subjects in Eeman's relaxation circuit, each one with left-hand connected with head (+) and right hand (+) with base of spine (–) of the other.

If rather than sensing progressive warmth, muscular relaxation, well-being and drowsiness, the subject senses restlessness and discomfort, then the polarities should be reversed, i.e. the left-hand should hold the lead connected to the spine, and the right hand should hold the lead connected to the head. Eeman states that in twenty-five years of testing many thousands of people he came across no more than half a dozen such 'wrong' reactions, and that even these returned to the normal relaxation circuit after three or four sessions on the otherwise 'tension inducing' circuit. No artificial energy is used in this method, i.e. nothing should be done to connect any part of the simple apparatus with any source of electricity. All that is being done is to place the individual into an 'electrical' or 'magnetic' circuit with himself, in a way which obviously benefits him. It is up to future researchers to establish exactly how this technique works.

Tapes and Teachers

There are literally hundreds of relaxation and meditation induction tapes on the market. Most of them take the listener verbally through the various stages of relaxation and the majority are useful and effective. Some may not succeed because the voice on the tape may irritate the listener. In many cases, the most successful voice to listen to is your own, and a number of books exist, from which you can read appropriate commentaries to aid this. Some tapes consist more of sounds and 'mood' music which enhances the relaxation state. Specific recommendations cannot be given, except to say that most people find these tapes helpful. The following sample induction commentaries may be recorded onto tape and played whenever necessary.

Sample Relaxation Sequence I (to be spoken *slowly* into a tape recorder).

Sit in a comfortable chair, keeping your spine straight.

I am sitting comfortably. My eyes are open but I shall be focusing on what takes place inside me. I am at peace with myself, safe and unhurried. My eyes are rolling upwards. My vision is blurred and out of focus. I can feel some strain in the muscles of my eyes. (Pause to experience this). I am looking upwards as far as I can. I can see my eyebrows. The strain is getting stronger. (Pause). I will keep looking upwards. When I blink it feels good.

If I close my eyes, the strain will ease. I am still looking upwards at my eyebrows. The strain is very strong. (Pause to experience this). I am closing my eyes. The ease and relaxation in the eye muscles is wonderful. The darkness of having my eyes closed is nice. The relaxation and release makes me feel good. This feeling of ease is spreading from my eyes, to my face, and neck and spine.

(Pause to experience this). I feel a general easing and relaxing spreading through my body. (Pause). My neck feels limp and supple. (Pause). My shoulders and arms are at ease and there is a heaviness spreading down my arms. (Pause to sense the heaviness. Repeat the phrase and pause again).

As I breathe in and out I feel I am more and more at ease. As I breathe in, the air brings with it health and energy. As I breathe out, I am aware of letting go, of becoming heavier. Each time I breathe out I feel heavier and more relaxed. I feel like taking a few deep breaths. As I breathe out I feel I am sinking into the chair. (Pause and repeat). My body is becoming heavier and I am sinking deeper. (Repeat and pause). My body feels relaxed and heavy. (Pause to sense the heaviness, repeat the phrase and pause again). My limbs are loose and limp and heavy. (Pause to sense this and then repeat the phrase). I feel safe and at one with myself. I feel at peace with life and totally relaxed. My limbs are heavy. (Pause and repeat). My whole body is heavy. (Pause and repeat). I feel warmth spreading throughout me. (Pause to experience this, repeat the phrase and pause again). I am heavy and warm and safe. (Pause to enjoy this, then repeat the phrase).

After a short while in this rested state, the following sequence should be listened to, i.e. allow a minute or two of silence on the tape and then record:

I am going to breathe deeply now. As I breathe in I feel energy and strength coming into my body. (Repeat several times). I feel alert and content. I feel I want to stretch my muscles (do so), and my whole body (do so). I am opening my eyes and I feel refreshed and alert and relaxed.

Altogether this should take about ten minutes. Phrases can be repeated as many times as you feel you want to in order to enhance particular feelings of warmth, heaviness, etc. Pauses should be kept for at least ten and up to twenty seconds to sense and savour particular feelings. If desired, the following sequence can follow on from the relaxation stage after the phrase 'I am heavy and warm and safe' and before commencing the return to wakeful alertness; alternatively, it can be used at a different time after a short introductory relaxation breathing exercise.

Sample Relaxation Sequence II

You will be sitting as before and after five to ten cycles of complete breathing, in which you have consciously allowed yourself to release all muscular tension of which you are aware, play a recording of the following (remembering to speak slowly):

I feel warm, relaxed and safe. (Repeat several times). I feel at peace with myself. I am descending slowly down a spiral staircase. I am going down, deeper and deeper down. I am looking down at the thick carpeting on the stairs which take me down and down and down. I feel comfortable and at ease as I go down the stairs. I feel warm and safe. I am going deeper and deeper, down and down. The peacefulness and quiet is wonderful. I love the quiet and peace. (Pause). I feel safe and at ease as I descend down the carpeted stairs. I feel warm, safe and relaxed. (Pause). I am near the bottom of the stairs and there is a doorway. I see the warm sunshine outside. I step into the golden glow of the sun and feel its embracing warmth. (Pause). I am walking across a meadow in the warm sunshine. I feel happy and safe. This is a beautiful place. I hear birds. (Pause). I see flowers. (Pause). I smell grass. (Pause). There is a river. By the river there is a rowing boat. I am lying in the boat and it is drifting gently on the river. The boat rocks gently as it drifts down the river. I feel safe. The sun is warm on me. The boat is drifting gently down the river. (Pause). I am completely relaxed and at peace. (Pause). I hear the water gently lapping. I feel the warm sun. I am at peace and safe and happy. (Pause). The boat is drifting gently towards the bank of the river. I feel safe and at peace and fully relaxed. The boat is gently rocking by the river bank. I step out of it and lie in the shade of a lovely tree. I am completely relaxed and happy and safe. (Pause). This is a beautiful place and a wonderful experience. I am warm and relaxed. (Pause for a minute to experience the peace, silence and relaxed state). It is time to go. I shall breathe deeply and open my eyes and be alert and refreshed.

This sequence can also take about ten minutes and may be used instead of or as well as those in the accompanying chapters.

Teachers

Teachers of relaxation and meditation methods can help in instructing the beginner. The Transcendental Meditation system is now almost universally available; most towns having a group teacher. This method has much to commend it and has the virtue of providing introductory courses for beginners as well as follow-up sessions to check on progress.

As far as stress-proofing is concerned, I would emphasize that meditation alone is not enough. It is certainly beneficial, and often dramatically effective in stress reduction but, by now, the reader should be aware that a more extensive programme is needed as well as meditation, discussion of which follows in the next chapter.

7.
Meditation

There are many forms of meditation and some will suit one individual more than another. It is therefore suggested that each method in this section be tried on a number of consecutive occasions, in order to fully assess its effect on you. Purists, and those who see meditation only in terms of spiritual development, would frown on this advice. There is the story of the pupil who had tried a variety of meditation methods and who, on approaching yet another teacher for advice, was told to lift a glass vial containing layers of coloured sand. Having shaken it as he was instructed, thus mixing all the layers into a grey mixture, the teacher admonished him: 'This is the effect on you of all these teachings. Each of them in their own way is pure, but look what has become of them inside you'.

In my experience, when using meditation in an attempt to reduce the effects of stress, some systems are better suited to particular personalities than others. The only way to discover what suits you is to try several methods and judge for yourself—or go to a teacher for guidance. Relaxation methods, as outlined in the previous chapter, should have been practised for some weeks before starting to introduce other meditation methods. There are a variety of ways of doing this, e.g.

1. Continue with the relaxation exercises twice daily and add one meditation session at a suitable time;

2. Replace one of the relaxation exercises with one of the meditation methods;

3. Do a short relaxation exercise, say for five minutes, followed by ten minutes of meditation, twice daily.

Whichever you choose, try to stick to the same meditation method for a week or so to assess whether it enables you to achieve the calmer, more alert state which is intended. What all meditation methods have in common is the conscious attempt to focus the mind on one object. In this respect, the relaxation methods already outlined could be seen as forms of meditation. The 'pure' meditation that it is hoped you will be able to add to one of the relaxation methods, provides a different dimension to the programme; for, whilst it is not too difficult to concentrate one's attention on the breathing mechanism and on counting whilst breathing, for example, it requires a greater degree of application to concentrate on an abstract thought or image. What is essential in meditation is a device through which the conscious mind can be diverted from everyday thought processes. In separating the relaxation exercises from meditation methods, I am aware that they do overlap. However, whilst meditation leads inevitably to relax-ation and *perhaps* to spiritual awareness, relaxation exercises can seldom lead to more than just relaxation, which is what we are seeking at this stage.

The device or 'distracting object' can be a mental picture or image, a word, a sound, a real object, an idea, an activity, etc. Whatever it is, all other thoughts must thereby be excluded from conscious awareness. There is a form of meditation in which no particular object is selected, but in which the individual attempts to focus on everything that is happening around himself, becoming as fully aware of his internal and external environment as possible during the meditation. This has been called 'open' meditation. All meditation involves a suspension of judgement. The object is observed non-critically. No thoughts about it are encouraged, simply a passive attention to the object. Some methods attempt to combine the use of an object (say breathing or a sound) and the 'open' pattern of meditation' in which thoughts entering the mind are 'watched' but not 'judged' and are then replaced by the meditative object. Research has shown that a variety of physiological changes take place during meditation. Certainly, tension and stress are reduced in the process. Frequently, behaviour patterns involving addiction, such as smoking, overeating and drug or alcohol consumption are improved or controlled by meditation. Such stress-induced conditions as high blood pressure are also markedly affected for the better by the application of successful meditation methods.

In general terms, meditation has been found to produce feelings of greater alertness and ability to concentrate, of being more perceptive, and so on. Many people experience an 'awakening' or a heightening of spiritual awareness. Supporters of these methods often use such phrases as 'cosmic consciousness' and 'transcendental experiences'. These phrases should not put off the would-be meditator for, at the very least, a greater sense of well-being and a more relaxed state should follow meditation. If any of the other benefits or experiences also follow, they should be taken as a bonus. Reduction in stress is difficult to measure. Frequently, the gradual, beneficial changes that do accrue are only measurable by comparison with the previous state of tension. Keeping a record of your results in the stress-assessment lists in Chapter 4 will enable you to make such a comparison after some months of regular relaxation and meditation.

The position or posture adopted for meditation is of importance. The classical poses range from the lotus position to the kneeling at prayer position. Most variations insist that during meditation the spine be kept straight, and this should be remembered, whether you decide to sit or kneel (perhaps using a small meditation stool), or even stand. Many systems and teachers have linked the way we hold and use our bodies with our emotional state. There seems to be a two-way influence, in as much as a physical symptom will usually develop in response to emotional stress, and emotions will be influenced by any tension or 'armouring' in the musculature.

Once the appropriate posture has been adopted, the mind should accept, initially, that you will stay immobile until the completion of the exercise. This stillness is an essential part of meditation and does itself lead to desirable physiological changes, as well as having positive psychological benefits such as increased self-respect and confidence. The self-discipline involved in immobility is enhanced if, during meditation, any irritant such as the buzzing of a fly or an aching of the limbs can be ignored or dismissed and the meditation process continued.

Figure 3

Three positions for meditation. Ideally the spine should remain straight throughout, however, should the head loll to one side during the exercise and the position still be one of ease, then this will not detract from the benefits.

It is known that the meditation experience increases with repetition. Regular meditation requires an element of self-discipline and organization. It is well worth the effort, and once it becomes a part of the daily routine, the oasis of calm and regeneration, which the meditation period brings, will be eagerly anticipated.

Choose a suitably unhurried part of the day to practise. Morning and evening seem to suit many people. Avoid meditating soon after meals, if possible. Adopt a sitting or kneeling position. (Lying is not suggested for meditation). Remember to keep the spine straight.

Method I: Concentration
The simplest and probably the oldest form of meditation

involves concentrating on one object. It has long been established that by allowing the eyes to roll upwards as you commence meditation, the effect is more speedily achieved. The head is erect and the eyes look upwards as far as they can (towards the eyebrows). This may be accompanied by mild muscular discomfort, which should pass. If this is not found to enhance any of the following methods, then close the eyes from the beginning. Normally, after a short while of maintaining the strained upward-rolled position of the eyes, it comes as a relief and a relaxing experience to gently close the eyes and to then continue the method with the eyes closed.

Breathing in a relaxed, unforced manner, focus the mind on an *imagined* object (a cross, a candle flame, a circle of light, etc.) or, with the eyes looking ahead, focus on an actual object of a similar nature; alternatively, with the eyes gently closed or rolled upwards, repeat a meaningless sound in the mind (not out loud). If visualizing an imaginary or gazing at a real object, simply dwell passively on it. Thoughts that intrude should be gently discarded and replaced by the image of the object on which you are concentrating. If a sound is being used ('om', 'aaah', etc.) this should be repeated rhythmically over and over again. It may take on its own rhythm, becoming a continuous drone. The most important point is that concentration should be held on the sound and not directed towards anything else.

Concentrative forms of meditation require persistent practice before they can be maintained for any length of time. At first, the beginner may find that it is not possible to maintain concentration on an image or object (imagined or real) for more than a few seconds at a time before thoughts intrude. Gradually, with patience and discipline, it will be found that minutes at a time will pass in this state and, finally, that it is possible to maintain concentration for as long as is required. This method, by focusing the mind, enhances relaxation, reduces anxiety, and frequently helps in the elimination of psychosomatic ailments. One example of concentrative meditation is a Hindu method known as *tratak*. The object of concentration in this method is a burning flame, which is placed at eye level about a foot in front of the meditator. Breathing is slow, deep and silent. The meditator gazes into the centre of the flame until tears begin to flow, at which point the eyes are closed, and the image of the flame is visualized until it too vanishes.

Another concentrative meditation is that used by raj yogi. They meditate with their eyes closed, focusing attention on the tip of the nose, or the back of the skull. Experiments on meditators who use these methods showed that very soon after starting meditation, alpha waves (a sign of a relaxed state) appeared, and that these were maintained without interruption, despite the following external stimuli being administered: loud banging noises; the meditator's hands being placed in cold water or being touched with a hot tube; bright light; vibration from a tuning fork, etc. In other words, the meditation process was so powerful that none of these stimuli could disturb it or its relaxing effect (as measured by alpha brain wave patterns).

When effectively performed, meditation which makes use of concentration, blots out all other sensations and thoughts. This is the key to its usefulness in stress-proofing, for with practice it becomes possible to focus the mind on one thing, be it a sound or an object, and detach oneself from all others. A few minutes in this silent state has restorative and relaxing effects. It is suggested that an attempt is made to spend ten minutes at a time performing such exercises, but that at first only a few minutes be attempted, perhaps tagged on to the end of a relaxation method.

Method II: Contemplation

In many ways this method is similar to the previous one. The object in the mind of the meditator can be an abstract idea, such as 'goodness', 'love', 'truth', etc. or the idea of God. Extension of this can be to use repetitive sounds or phrases, which are repeated rhythmically and silently, for example, 'God is love', or 'Hail Mary full of Grace, the Lord is with thee', etc. Any meaningful phrase will do. As long as the repeated phrase occupies the mind totally, it will have its effect. The constant barrage of thoughts and images, most of them meaningless and useless, that usually occupy our minds needs to be stilled, and these methods are designed to achieve this. The individual's view of the world and of himself, may well be altered as a result, sometimes for only a short time and sometimes permanently.

For those who would rather avoid religious connotations during meditation, the suggestion of Krishnamurti, the Indian philosopher, is that the sound to be repeated could well be 'coca-cola, coca-cola'. There is certainly no reason why this should not be as effective as any other object or sound in silencing thought. Although there are those who maintain that the content and vibrational quality of the 'mantra' or repeated words or sounds, determines their effect, research has tended to support the idea that it is the *act* of repetition and not the actual sound that produces the desired result, at least in so far as relaxation is concerned. Herbert Benson M.D., author of *Relaxation Response*, says that the repeated word 'bananas' will do the trick. This, of course, may be seen as an affront to the spiritual connotations of meditating, but in so far as it is our concern to achieve relaxation, 'bananas' or 'coca-cola' would do as well as anything else. After ten minutes of this, allow the mind to become aware of the surroundings and how you feel, and then open the eyes, stretch the body and return to normal activities.

Method III: Meditating on 'Bubbles' of Thought

Adopt the desired position and induce a state of relaxation. See the mind as the surface of a pond, smooth and calm. Thoughts that enter the mind should be seen as bubbles rising from the depths of the pond. They should be observed, not pursued. In other words, the deliberate following of the thought process is avoided. Simply *detach* yourself and observe your thoughts as they 'bubble' to the surface. Take note of the thought and then gently, without any force, return to your contemplation of the smooth surface of the pond. It is also possible to sink under the surface of the pond, into deeper layers of consciousness as time goes by. As long as thoughts are not intrusive, but are observed and then depart' just like the bubbles, the meditation process is continuing. After ten minutes or so, allow the mind to focus on the immediate environment; sense a degree of relaxation and then end the session.

Method IV: Meditating on Your Corner of Heaven
In this method, after adopting an initial posture and relaxing consciously, with the eyes closed or rolled upwards, begin to visualize a place in which you would feel happy and safe. This could be a real, remembered place. It could be a room or a country or garden scene, or any other place to which you could go whenever you wanted peace and a feeling of security. This place should be so visualized (imagined in the mind's eye) that it can be stepped into and out of as though entering a picture. The picture can be added to as time goes by. If it is a room, then furnishings can be changed or added to or rearranged. Colours should be seen and, if possible, all the senses should gradually be brought into the meditation. Try to hear the sounds (e.g. clocks ticking, bird songs, etc.); smell the various odours (a log fire, newly mown grass, flowers); feel the textures (bark of the tree, velvet upholstery), and so on. There is no limit to the degree of embroidery that is possible in creating this special place. All the powers of your imagination should be employed. This sort of meditation has been called creating a 'safe harbour', and it should be seen by the meditator, whilst conscious of its imagined nature, to be useful as a retreat whenever it is required. This meditation employs all the senses, and is suitable for many who find it too difficult a task to maintain concentration on one object. After ten minutes or so, the meditator steps out of the picture and returns to the normal environment, knowing that the 'safe place' remains untouched and ready for the next visit.

Whichever method of meditation suits you best, it is suggested that you construct such a 'safe haven' for yourself anyway, as it is a valuable exercise in imagery, and is of great use in visualization techniques (see the following chapter).

Method V: Breathing and Colour Visualization
Adopt a reclining or sitting position of comfort in an appropriate room. Breathe deeply several times and sense a feeling of safe, warm ease. Continue to breathe slowly and deeply, but not in a straining manner. As you breathe, visualize the colours red, orange and yellow flowing upwards into your solar plexus. These hues should be visualized one at a time and seen as rivers of colour. The breathing rhythm should not be

controlled, but should be allowed to find its own pace and depth. The colours should be seen to flow at a steady, unhurried pace. After spending a minute or so on each of the first three colours, visualize the colour green flowing into the solar plexus from directly in front of you. Spend a minute or so breathing in a slow, rhythmic manner with the image of a river of green light entering your body.

Follow this with blue, indigo and violet, one at a time; these should be seen as being breathed inwards from the air above you. Again, spend a minute or so visualizing each of these colours. The only problem presented by this method is the difficulty some people have in visualizing colours. This becomes easier with practice, although some colours will always be easier to 'see' than others. After completing the colour spectrum, see yourself as being bathed in blue light, and end the meditation with a deep sense of peace and calm before opening the eyes and resuming normal activities.

Method VI: Tactile Meditation

This method employs the sense of touch to help procure the meditative state. The requirements for this are either a set of 'worry beads' or four or five pebbles. Adopt a relaxed posture, keeping the spine straight, and consciously 'let go' of any muscular tensions. Hold the beads gently in one hand and, with the other, rhythmically and methodically move them between your fingers, touching them one at a time. As each bead is moved, it should be felt and counted. It is helpful to have a slow, rhythmical count, up to about five; this is then repeated over and over. Count, handle and 'hear' the beads – one, two, three, four, five. The same effect can be achieved by passing pebbles from one hand to the other. Feel, sense and count them, focusing all the attention on this slow, repetitive movement. After ten minutes, open the eyes and resume your normal activities.

Method VII: Attention to Life

This is not a method to be used at the daily or twice daily relaxation-meditation sessions, but rather during normal activities. The objective is to consciously focus all the attention on the particular moment, activity or task. If a mundane activity is selected for this treatment, then a focusing on all aspects of it is required. Let us take a task such as washing the hands or face. The eyes should be closed and all the senses employed to feel and register everything about this simple act. Such sensations as soap being lathered on wet hands, the feel, sound, smell and temperature changes of the whole procedure, should be focused on and registered as acutely as possible. Whatever the particular action chosen (and it is a good idea to pick several, short actions each day), the effect is to heighten awareness, and to encourage a feeling of being fully in the 'here and now' rather than doing such everyday tasks whilst thinking about other things. In time, it will become possible to concentrate on the present for longer and longer periods.

This type of meditation requires that the individual first consciously relaxes all muscles, apart from those essential to the task, and that only enough muscular effort is used to ensure its successful completion. Whether the task is peeling a piece of fruit or a vegetable, or making a bed, or driving a car, or writing a letter, what is essential is that all the senses be employed, and that total application of the mind is to that task alone. All other thoughts and concerns should be ignored. If you can learn to focus totally on present time, albeit for short periods, you will begin to reduce the amount of stress factors which are constantly at work. You will do whatever you have to do more efficiently, with greater satisfaction and less effort. This is one of the values of a truly absorbing hobby, be it music, painting, gardening or anything else – it is so beneficial in terms of reducing stress.

Note: All meditation methods will assist in achieving relaxation; indeed, meditation is not possible without it. There is no right or wrong way of meditating, as long as the conscious mind is being stilled. If you come across any difficulties, take advice from a teacher of these methods.

8.
Using the Power of
the Mind for Healing

There is overwhelming evidence that much of the illness suffered by mankind results to some extent, from stress and emotional causes. The evidence for the reversal of such illness by means of a shift in the psychological make-up (beliefs, attitudes, etc.) of the individual, together with stress reduction, is becoming equally overwhelming. Logically enough, it is necessary for the individual to use images and ideas that make sense to himself when attempting to reverse a process that has caused his illness. A complicated scientific explanation of the mind's activities is not always of great use to the person involved. In the simplest terms possible, therefore, as well as learning a basic relaxation method, self-healing by these means involves the person in:

1. Believing that he can be better; 2. Seeing himself getting better; 3. Visualizing, in terms that make sense to himself, the actual disease process being overcome by the body.

The Simontons, in their excellent book *Getting Well Again* (Bantam Books), describe the changes which they have observed in the upward spiral towards recovery. It is as well to realize that their work has dealt mainly with that most dreaded of diseases, cancer. Even so, they have observed the healing power of the mind operating in numerous individuals who have controlled or overcome their disease. If this is true of cancer, then it can be applied to any reversible health problem, chronic or acute.

Firstly, say the Simontons, it is noticeable that with the diagnosis of a life-threatening disease, the individual appears to gain new perspectives on his or her problems. Further, the threat to life seems to release them from previous behaviour patterns into which they were locked by habit (for example, hostility, long suppressed, can now be expressed etc.). Often, personality changes occur, through which old attitudes and rules of conduct are suspended, and unresolved conflicts show signs of resolution. These changes are accompanied by a lifting of depression and greater psychological energy. It is as though, in these people, the disease has given them permission to change. As hope and a greater desire to live begin to operate, physical changes begin to be felt, and these reinforce the positive changes in the psychological state. Eventually, with recovery, the individual often enjoys better health than ever before.

How can this sort of change be encouraged and enhanced? It is by no means the norm, but is nevertheless seen in many of those patients who did overcome their illness. If such changes could be included in the programme of treatment for all in ill health, what a revolution it would cause. As already mentioned, in order to consciously employ such knowledge to one's advantage, the individual must use his own belief system. In order to do this effectively, a brief outline is necessary of how altered attitudes and the techniques of visualization and 'guided imagery' can reinforce the process.

Psychological stress, resulting in depression and despair, acts through the brain to negatively influence the body's defence and control systems (immune system, hormonal activity, etc.), resulting in inadequate protection and breakdown in normal health. In such a case, a variety of other variables, ranging from inherited factors to nutritional and structural factors, will determine just what parts of the body begin to malfunction and become diseased.

The reversal of this process, if it is to be effective, needs to begin on the psychological level, thus influencing the brain centres (limbic system, hypothalamus, etc.) which determine hormonal and immune system function and thus the healing process. The simple answer then, is that hope and anticipation of recovery need to be linked with altered attitudes and reduced anxiety (relaxation exercises, etc.). From a holistic viewpoint, all other aspects of health, for instance, diet and exercise, should also at this point be corrected. The relaxation exercises and simple meditation methods previously presented, will have opened the way for further use of the power of the mind in the healing process. The guided imagery or visualization methods which are outlined below, show how to make use of the mind's power. The individual should vary the images and phrases to suit his own needs.

Method 1

Use the relaxation method that most suits you in order, within a few minutes, to induce a sense of ease. This could be a breathing technique or progressive muscular relaxation, etc. (see Chapter 6). Use the 'safe haven' meditation (page 115) in order to spend two or three minutes in safe, peaceful and harmonious contemplation. You are now ready for guided visualization to promote healing. Create in your mind a picture of any illness or ailment you have. This should be done in a way that makes sense to you. It does not have to be scientifically accurate. Examples will be given below of how this might be done.

Having visualized your ailment, illness or condition, try to visualize your body's defence and healing mechanisms over-coming, controlling or correcting the condition. It is as well to keep firmly in mind that there are few, if any, conditions which cannot be improved, controlled or normalized by virtue of the self-healing mechanisms of the body. If any treatment is being undertaken to help the condition, visualize this, too, in whatever way makes sense to you. See the body healing and normalizing the problem with the aid of whatever treatment you are having. *Know* that you will be well again.

See yourself well, healthy, free of pain or discomfort; visualize yourself being active and doing something pleasant, such as walking in a meadow or swimming in the sea. Visualize yourself achieving something you have as a goal in life. Feel satisfied and content that you are, in this way, able to support and participate consciously in your recovery.

When you have completed the visualization, either rest for a while or resume your normal activities. Do this exercise two or three times daily, as well as or instead of your relaxation programme. 5 to 10 minutes of this imagery should be performed on each occasion.

Examples of visualization of illnesses or problems, and how your body and treatment will be able to overcome them are as follows:

1. *Painful area, joint, muscle, etc. (e.g. arthritis, rheumatism)*
See the area and visualize the blood vessels as being congested with dark red blood; see the tense, inflamed muscles and the irritated joint surfaces. Now see fresh, pink, oxygen-rich blood, full of healing white blood cells, flushing though the blood vessels, carrying away the rough deposits, relaxing the tense muscles. Visualize the area again, but this time, see it as relaxed, free of congestion and with no crystals, just smooth, polished joint surfaces and healthy pink muscles and blood. See the joint and muscles performing their normal functions, such as running, lifting, bending, etc.

2. *An open wound or ulcer:* Picture the area and see the raw, inflamed tissues. Visualize the blood stream gently covering the area with a soothing lining of protective cells. See them proliferating and dividing to form new, healthy tissue. See the wound covered and normal. See yourself well and healthy and free of pain.

3. *A bronchial problem:* See the lungs and its network of tubes being irritated by mucous deposits. See the mucus being cleared away by the body, and see the air passages clearing and expanding to allow a free passage of air. Visualize the removed debris being easily coughed up and then picture the soft mucous membrane lining the air passages and producing just enough clear liquid to lubricate the movement of the surfaces. See the lungs expanding to their full capacity. See yourself walking, running or enjoying any activity which at present might be difficult.

4. *Circulatory problems:* See the narrowed blood vessels and imagine them constricted and perhaps partly obstructed. Visualize the body, aided by any treatment you are undergoing, as dilating the blood vessels, clearing away any obstructions and relaxing the small muscles which contract the vessels. See fresh, healthy blood flushing through the arteries. See areas, normally deprived of blood, as flushed and warm. The detail of how this takes place is irrelevant. What matters is that you see something take place which will lead to the desired state. The deposits in the blood vessels can be seen as a chalky lining.

The removal can be seen as a melting or chipping away by the body's defence mechanism, represented in your visualization by white blood cells which can be pictured as soldiers or an army of workers. The more graphic and real the images, the better. In dealing with such serious problems as cancer, these methods are extremely helpful. Some cancer patients learn to visualize the tumour cells as grey, soft masses which are attacked by this white blood-cell army and destroyed. The white cells can be pictured as knights on horseback, or soldiers carrying flame throwers or as woodsmen carrying axes, etc. The more vivid the picture of the body fighting and overcoming the enemy, the better. *It does not need to be based on scientific fact*, but should be associated, in your own mind, with the ailment you are treating.

Any ailment or condition can be approached this way and negative thoughts, doubts and fears can thus be overcome. A sense of being in control of the healing process brings with it self-confidence and hope; the will to live, the determination not to give in, the knowledge that you are working *with* your body, and *with* the healing process – all these factors are enhanced, and are of immeasurable value. Real physical changes can stem directly from 'guided imagery' of this type. Believing in one's recovery makes it all the more likely and speeds up the process.

It is not possible for everyone to visualize pictures of the sort described. In some cases, people just cannot think in this way and in such cases, verbal images or 'feelings', are perfectly adequate. Remember that the exercise is flexible enough to be used by anyone. It is a matter of seeing the problem *your* way and imagining the way in which the body, sustained by treatment, may overcome it. All this should be images, words or feelings that make sense to you.

The images you select and the meaning that they hold for you are of importance. In this respect, it is worth emphasizing that (1) the illness must be seen as a weak, vulnerable enemy; (2) the body's defence capacity must be seen as strong and easily capable of destroying and removing the enemy (deposits in arteries, arthritic deposits, tumour cells, etc.); (3) previously damaged areas are thought of as easily repaired by the body and should be seen as normal again; (4) any debris from the healing process is thought of as easily cleared from the body and should be seen as flushed away; (5) any treatment should be seen as supportive of the powerful healing mechanisms, and providing an even more certain end to the problem.

Method II

Whereas method I is suitable for promoting recovery from or control of actual illness, this method is aimed at improving health and function in a person who shows no obvious signs of illness. The aim might be to achieve that extra dimension of health and well-being that most people never reach. Extra vitality and energy might be another aim. A slimmer more supple body might be another. Initially, therefore, you must have in your mind the ideal state which you seek. Use the relaxation method that most suits you in order, within a few minutes, to induce a sense of ease. This could be a breathing technique or the progressive muscular relaxation exercise (see Chapter 6). Use the 'safe haven' meditation (see page 115) in order to spend two or three minutes in peaceful and harmonious contemplation. You are now ready for a creative visualization exercise.

Visualize or imagine the desired state exactly as you wish it to be. (You are slimmer, more energetic, or your hair is thick and silky, etc.). If it relates to your ability to deal with others, see yourself in a situation which might previously have bothered you, but which you visualize in the exercise as being easily coped with. Everything proceeds easily and smoothly; you are confident and relaxed.

Retain the image or idea you wish to promote, strongly in the mind. To this picture add appropriate affirmative statements (silently or out loud). For example, 'I am slim and supple and healthy'; 'I feel energetic and full of vitality'; 'My body is strong, energetic and well'; 'I am happy and relaxed all the time', and so on.

These or other appropriate affirmations, which you repeat to yourself, are most important since they can have a physiological effect. (Recall the effect on the body of the affirmation 'my arm is getting warmer' in the autogenic training exercise). It is also important that such statements are not of a negative nature; for instance, do not say, 'I no longer feel tired', but say

'I feel wide awake and energetic'. It is also important that the statement sounds right to you, and thus fulfils the role that it should.

After a few minutes of visualizing the desired goal, and then affirming it with positive statements, remind yourself that the goal you seek is the normal and natural state, to which we are all entitled, that the relaxation and visualization method is removing obstacles and blockages which might have been preventing this desired natural state from occurring. In this way, you mentally affirm that what you seek is not a wild, preposterous dream, but a reasonable and natural expectation.

Visualize the vital energy of life coursing through and see it in whatever terms make sense to you. See health as an energy which glows, warm and golden, and which bathes and succours you. Feel its warmth and see its glow as you are surrounded and bathed by this vital force, which your relaxed state is opening you to. If transient thoughts or negative doubts intrude, just repeat your appropriate affirmation – which you should have decided on in advance – or visualize your desired goal, or see and feel the energy previously described. Continue with this for as long as you wish; not less than five and not more than twenty minutes is probably a reasonable range of times to be guided by. The various aspects of the exercise can also be repeated as often as you wish.

Needless to say, it is desirable that, in conjunction with such a visualization programme, you actually do things to enhance the likelihood of success, whether this involves eating a balanced diet, getting enough exercise, etc.). These exercises in visualization are relaxing and health-promoting extensions of the exercises described in the chapters on relaxation and meditation.

By applying, as appropriate, methods I and II, the innate self-healing capacity of the body is allowed to operate. This is not something you can force, but by passive attention to the positive images and ideas employed, you are creating a situation in which the desired outcome becomes more probable. By altering one's attitudes, coming to believe that healing and recovery are going to take place, and by giving the mind and body the chance to accomplish its self-regulating, homeostatic endeavours, profound changes can occur. The power of the mind, when harnessed to positive goals which the individual *believes* are attainable, can transform a sick person to a well one, and a well person to a positively healthy one.

Index